Stillness
IN A
WORLD FULL
OF TURMOIL

Also by Msgr. Laurence Spiteri
from Sophia Institute Press:

Canon Law Explained

Msgr. Laurence J. Spiteri, J.C.D, Ph.D.

Stillness
IN A
WORLD FULL
OF TURMOIL

SOPHIA INSTITUTE PRESS
Manchester, New Hampshire

Nihil obstat: Raffaele Cardinal Farina, S.D.B.,
Cardinal emeritus librarian and archivist of the Roman Church,
Vatican City, Censor, January 3, 2022

Imprimatur: Mauro Cardinal Gambetti, O.F.M. Conv.,
Vicar General of His Holiness, Vatican City, January 3, 2022

The *nihil obstat* and *imprimatur* are official declarations that a book or pamphlet is free of doctrinal or moral error. No implication is contained therein that those who have granted the *nihil obstat* and *imprimatur* agree with the contents, opinions or statements expressed.

Sophia Institute Press
Box 5284, Manchester, NH 03108
1-800-888-9344
www.SophiaInstitute.com

Sophia Institute Press is a registered trademark of Sophia Institute.

paperback ISBN 978-1-64413-856-4

ebook ISBN 978-1-64413-857-1

Library of Congress Control Number: 2023934029

First printing

I dedicate this book to Our Lady,
consoler of her children.

Contents

Prologue

I am delighted to write the introduction to Msgr. Laurence Spiteri's latest book entitled *Stillness in a World Full of Turmoil*. This is a book where the pastoral heart of a priest speaks to the heart of God's people. It is not only rooted in his priestly ministry of the written word but particularly in Sacred Scripture. Msgr. Spiteri's profound knowledge of Sacred Scripture enabled him to provide 499 references to the Bible and apply them to daily life. This is another time where the author exhibits the special gift of presenting very complicated themes in a forthright choice of words that are understandable to every person in a way where the scriptural, doctrinal, and theological nuances are not lost on the reader.

A perusal glance at each title of the seven chapters in this book reveals that Msgr. Spiteri has touched on many contemporary issues in our lives as we live through the drama of Covid-19, its mutations and aftermath, and, most unfortunately, its reemergence. By applying Sacred Scripture to situations presented in everyday living, the author offers us the virtue of hope. The author provides his reader not only with Sacred Scripture insights, but also with themes that cover catechesis, sacramentology, patrology, spirituality, and Mariology as they relate to living in our world immersed in turmoil and our souls seeking tranquility. The author weaves a narrative that points to the answer of our search: stillness in God.

I congratulate Msgr. Spiteri for this wonderful book. Its reader will surely benefit greatly in finding inspiration, practical application of the tenets of our wonderful Catholic Faith, and hope in a world full of anxieties. May the reader find in his or her heart a stillness in the Lord, a peaceful resting in God that all of us surely need.

Raffaele Cardinal Farina, S.D.B.
Cardinal emeritus librarian and archivist
Vatican City, July 7, 2022

Stillness

IN A
WORLD FULL
OF TURMOIL

1

Who Are We?

What Makes Us Catholic?

Identity is one of the most important things necessary for our overall well-being. It reveals our individuality and uniqueness. It makes us claim that which is properly our very own and distinguishes us from others in that we are able to say, "I am me," and "You are you," and "This is mine," and "That is yours." It sets a boundary around us and serves as an invisible line of demarcation between our very self and that which belongs to other individuals. It provides us with self-awareness, as well as ascertains our specific status at home and within society. This does not only apply to an individual's personal identity, but also to the identity of a group of people as a unit—one's community. On the other hand, just as there is an identity within a physical community, so there is a personal identity in the spiritual sphere.

There are times when someone changes his or her spiritual identity and we hear the soul-shaking words: "I am no longer Catholic"; "I left the Church"; "I was hurt"; "The priest was mean to me"; "The bishop does not know that he is mixing religion with politics"; "There are many scandals in the Catholic Church"; and so forth. Thus, one turns in the old spiritual passport for a new and different one. This kind of reasoning sounds like a thought-out excuse to leave the Catholic Church, rather than a real reason for departure. These statements, nonetheless, should make us very concerned about the speaker, even more so when there is the case of departing for a non-Christian religion and the renunciation of Christ, whether explicit or implicit. I am absolutely sure that if one really knows what the Catholic Church is all about, one will never contemplate leaving her fold! Thus, in the great majority of cases, one is rejecting one's own *idea* of what the Catholic Church is.

In truth, the Catholic Church as a community of believers navigates the violent waves on an inclement ocean of worldly things that buffet around her with ephemeral promises, scandals, betrayals, defections, malfeasance, unfounded accusations, contempt, accusations of being out of touch with the times, counterfeit teachings, and demoralizing attacks—both from within and outside the Church. We should never be surprised because the Catholic Church has experienced this from her very beginning. Legend has it that, during a meeting between Napoleon Bonaparte and the Vatican's secretary of state, Ercole Cardinal Consalvi, the French emperor threatened to destroy the Catholic Church. Cardinal Consalvi coolly replied: "We clergy have been trying to destroy the Church for eighteen hundred years. What makes you think you'll do any better?" There are times when individuals at all levels of the Church succumb; they are never rejected or abandoned when they seek God's mercy. Instead, they are forgiven and accepted back with open arms and, hopefully, their souls find rest, as we see in the Parable of the Prodigal Son.[1]

---

[1] Luke 15:11–22.

The issue the majority of times is not about the Catholic Church as such, but, as already indicated, my and your thoughts and ideas of what exactly the Catholic Church *is*. Is she comprised solely of the pope, the bishops, the priests, and the religious? No! The Church is much bigger than all these things. The Catholic Church is much greater than our parish, our diocese, the world!

The Church is composed of three layers: the Church in Heaven, which will last for all eternity; the Church in Purgatory; and the Church on earth. The last two realities are temporal and will disappear when earthly human life completely stops. So, when someone says that he or she has left the Catholic Church, are they really saying that they do not want to be a member of the Church in Heaven? I doubt it!

There are instances when one abandons the Catholic Church because of deep devastating hurt or grave disappointment and disillusionment. This is always very tragic, but also very real. I am referring especially to victims of sexual abuse by members of the clergy. Such people and their loved ones have a most justifiable cause to be hurt and disillusioned, for they are gravely wounded. However, the Church wants them to stay in our household of God so that their healing and recovery would take place within and assisted by the Catholic community.

So, what exactly is the Catholic Church? A set of rules called the Catholic moral code? No, she is much more. A set of ecclesiastical regulations and laws that one must obey? No, she is bigger than that, too! A set of uniform beliefs that we are all bound to profess and live by? We're getting closer.

The Catholic Church professes a set of core beliefs that are called the *Deposit of Faith* and are not open for negotiation. Yet there are also other kinds of beliefs that do not specifically belong to the Deposit of Faith, but they do help us in our spiritual journey.

For example, private revelations, such as those of the Sacred Heart or Fátima or Lourdes, can inflame our hearts to live a deeper Christian life. These are not part of divine revelation that binds all Catholics, however.

The core beliefs, the Deposit of Faith, identify us as members of the Catholic Church. But this faith demands more from us than mere assent to certain points of doctrine. As Pope St. Gregory the Great (570–604) wrote some fifteen hundred years ago: "I assure you that it is not by faith that you will come to know Him, but by love; not by mere conviction, but by action."[2]

The Catholic Church on earth is a living community of believers who are the People of God. Pope Francis stated on June 12, 2013, that "being the Church, to be the People of God, in accordance with the Father's great design of love, means to be the leaven of God in this humanity of ours. It means to proclaim and to bring God's salvation to this world of ours, so often led astray, in need of answers that give courage, hope and new vigour for the journey."[3]

Each Catholic individual is personally called by God to be a Catholic. This is not coincidence or custom, as it might seem if our family and ancestors had always been Catholic. Rather, it is a matter of divine providence, which manifests itself down the centuries. Since Jesus Christ personally established the Church, He also calls each and every one of us to follow Him. You and I are individually and personally called to be Christian, and specifically to be Catholic. It is not some impersonal invitation. He chooses each one of us to be and to live as His brother or sister. Let us imagine ourselves being in a huge crowd and someone looking for us. How can the seeker find us? By calling us by name. Our

---

[2] St. Gregory the Great, Homily 14:3.
[3] Pope Francis, General Audience (June 12, 2013), no. 5.

personal name identifies and distinguishes us in the crowd. In a similar way, we belong to the huge crowd of humanity, and God calls us by our name. God singles us out.

Now, the act of being baptized makes us Christian. Many times, Catholics do not see themselves as being Christian! *Christian* is a rather generic term. We need to be specific. *Christian* is our first name, and *Catholic* is our last name. So, what is it exactly that makes us Catholic? Well, it comes in two ways: one way is that our parents and godparents took us as infants to the Catholic Church to be baptized. God called us and brings us to Himself through them. Or it happens when one who grew up in another faith tradition, or no faith at all, feels drawn to the Catholic Church. This person will then formally study the Catholic Faith and be received into her fold, either through Baptism for those never baptized or not baptized validly, or through a profession of the Catholic Faith for those already validly baptized in another Christian community. The second way usually takes place during the Easter Vigil, at the end of a period of formal instruction and a deeper discernment process. My personal experience as a priest is that the quality of the faith of a cradle Catholic is quite different than that of an adult convert to our Faith. The latter, admitting my shame, is more alive and committed than that of my "cradle" faith.

The Catholic Church was established by Jesus Christ[4] not because we are saints, but specifically because we are sinners. When I look at my life, I am always consoled by the fact that Jesus founded His Church on St. Peter, a self-proclaimed sinner[5] with many personal imperfections and foibles. It seems this truth is seldom remembered and, consequently, we look for perfect people within

---

[4]   Matt. 16:18.
[5]   Luke 5:8.

the Catholic Church, especially perfect spiritual leaders. But all of us are sinners on the way to becoming saints. All of us are broken, trying to be made spiritually healthy. None of us is exempt from the sacramental confession of our sins, not even the pope.

This does not mean that more should not be expected of our spiritual leaders. Yes, the clergy, from the newly ordained priest up to the pope, should be held to a higher standard. However, we should remember that all of us fall, be it occasionally or frequently, and, most unfortunately, some fall very hard, as the disheartening and very sad events have revealed in these last twenty years or so.

I am weak. You are weak. Those who say that they are not weak are simply fooling themselves.

The Catholic Church was established so that the Lord may walk hand in hand with each one of us on our personal life journey. To do so, He remains in our midst. He lives in our company, sinners though we are. He is not like a driving instructor who teaches us the mechanics of driving a car and the rules of the road and then tells us to follow them and off we go on our own. Rather, Jesus remains with us all the time. He is with us constantly, not only in spirit or by some personal recollection, such as when we feel that a deceased love one is next to us. Rather, He remains with us in His fullness: Body, Blood, soul, and divinity. This kind of existence is called the Real Presence—the Holy Eucharist.

The vision of the Catholic Church of the late Pope Benedict XVI is essentially eucharistic, for he taught that the Church is founded on the Holy Eucharist. In this regard, he based his argument on St. Paul's First Letter to the Corinthians, in which the apostle to the Gentiles taught that the members of the Church become the one Body of Christ by sharing in His eucharistic Body.

In other words, the Church and the eucharistic Christ are one and the same. Because there is no division in the Holy Eucharist, we are called to a deep communion with the Lord Jesus and with one another. According to Benedict (who was a first-class theologian), this identity of the Church and the eucharistic Lord emphasizes the Church as a communion, for she is united by the Sacred Scripture and the sacraments. She is one body, united vertically with the Trinity, and on the horizontal level her members are united with one another.

From ancient times, the Church (in Greek, *ekklesia*) saw the Holy Mass as her center. She is neither a club nor a group of friends, but the New People of God. There is only one Church. She exists in local church communities of the faithful that are united in the one Body of Jesus Christ, with each local community united with its bishop. The bishops and the dioceses entrusted to their respective pastoral care are united with one another and with the Bishop of Rome as the supreme leader, forming the one Catholic Church across the world. No local church is independent of the rest of the other local churches. Just think of the cells of our body—none of them are independent, and when there is an independent cell, there is the presence of illness.

This reasoning of universal communion in the Church leads the theologian-pope to emphasize the indispensable historical apostolic succession through validly ordained bishops, which links in an unbreakable bond the Church of today to the Church of the apostles. This succession ensures that the eucharistic Lord of two thousand years ago is the same eucharistic Lord present today. Furthermore, the Kingdom of God is never separate from Christ Himself or from the Church, for Christ and the Church are one. Therefore, when one truly, rather than emotionally, leaves the Catholic Church to join a non-Christian community, one separates not only from the Church but from Christ Himself. I believe that no one in his or her right mind intends to do such a thing.

The Catholic Church is the world's oldest institution, of any kind. She enjoys a continuity of identity, one Faith, and common structure that reaches back to the apostolic times. The lamentable fractures that exist in today's Christianity, for a variety of regrettable reasons, cannot deny the fact that non-Catholic Christian communities owe part of their own nature as a Christian community to their respective direct or indirect relationships with the Catholic Church.

The word *catholic*, we know, means "universal." And that is what the Catholic Church is. She is universal, international. She links local Catholics into one global communion under the pope, the successor to St. Peter. The mission that the Lord entrusted to His Church in her origins continues, for she wishes to mother more children and to make them part of her family on earth. This can be achieved through ecumenical efforts and missionary activity.

Now, what do I believe as a Catholic? I think that many a time we have a vague idea or some minimal idea of what we believe as Catholics. We might think that going to church makes us Catholic. This is something honorable but not precise, because many non-Catholics go to a Catholic Church—say a Jewish or Protestant spouse goes to church with his or her Catholic family members. We all know that his or her going to church does not make him or her Catholic. What is it then that makes us Catholic?

In order to answer this question, we have to go back to the time when Jesus established the Church. He said to St. Peter, "You are Peter, and on this rock I will build my Church, and the powers of death shall not prevail against it."[6] Then, Jesus went ahead and, after His Resurrection and Ascension into Heaven, sent the Holy Spirit at the first Pentecost and established the Church on earth. Now, that was a very interesting event, for the Acts of the Apostles

[6] Matt. 16:18.

informs us that the Holy Spirit descended upon all those, as individuals and as a unit, who were in the Upper Room—the room in which ancient tradition informs us that the Lord celebrated His Last Supper and instituted the Holy Eucharist, by which He remains in our company. In that Upper Room at Pentecost there were present not only the apostles, but also other disciples of the Lord. And what is most interesting is that there was also present Our Lady. The Holy Spirit who descended upon her thirty-four years previously at the moment of the conception of the second Person of the Trinity as man—at the Incarnation—is the same One who descended to establish the Church. Our Lady was not exempt from being a member of the Church just because she was the Mother of Jesus Christ. She, too, is a member of the Church. This is the same Church to which you and I belong.

To reiterate, it is a Church whose members as Catholic individuals are united in one faith and uniform beliefs with the other members of their parish. Each parish is in unity with the other parishes that together form a diocese and are under the ministerial service of their local bishop. Each diocese is in union with the other dioceses across the world, just as each bishop is in union with the rest of the bishops. All members are in union with the Bishop of Rome as the universal head and shepherd of the Catholic Church.

There may be a number of ways to express our fidelity to Jesus Christ. Therefore, we should move away from the secular notions of conservative or liberal or any other similar and divisive labels. The Catholic Church is not a political party or a philosophical society. The real issue that counts is being faithful to the Lord as members of the Catholic Church.

Pope Francis has a very interesting way of describing a Catholic. He expects each Catholic to carry an identity card—namely, "the Gospel's joy, the joy of having been chosen by Jesus, saved by Jesus, regenerated by Jesus; the joy of that hope that Jesus is waiting for us, the joy that—even with the crosses and sufferings we bear in this life—is expressed in another way, which is peace in the certainty that Jesus accompanies us, is with us."[7] That identity card was given to us at Baptism. Does anyone want to tear it up by leaving the Catholic Church? We belong, we struggle, we fall, we disappoint, we are imperfect, we sin, yet we are not abandoned by a forgiving and merciful Father-God. We always have our brother Jesus, who spilled His Blood on the Cross for us, and our loving mother Mary—not to mention all the glorious family of saints in Heaven, a Church through whom God seeks to make saints out of sinners.

Our God-Given Patrimony

St. Paul said, "Woe to me if I do not preach the Gospel!"[8] Not handing on the good news—our Catholic Faith—to the next generation will also be our undoing.

Pope Emeritus Benedict XVI (2005–2013), while still ministering as the Bishop of Rome, called for a new evangelization in the universal Church. Two great events marked this summons: the inauguration of the *Year of Faith* on October 11, 2012, and the convocation of the Thirteenth Ordinary General Assembly of the Synod of Bishops during the same month, focusing on the new evangelization. The Synod was entitled "The New Evangelization for the Transmission of the Christian Faith." The pope invited the Catholic faithful across the world to meet the Lord anew and to rediscover the rich heritage entrusted to all of us. Even before he was elected pope in 2005, Benedict was

---

[7] Pope Francis, Homily at Casa Santa Marta (June 9, 2014).
[8] 1 Cor. 9:16.

convinced that relativism was (and remains) a dreadful assault on the Church, for this philosophy holds no absolute and unalterable truths and, consequently, no perennial moral values, and leads to totalitarianism and temporary values dictated by a majority vote that change with the passage of time and new configurations of a community.

I am fully committed to Benedict's call to re-evangelize ourselves, relearn the Deposit of Faith, recommit ourselves to the Lord Jesus, rededicate ourselves to the Church that He established on earth, and hold on to divinely revealed truths, which have no expiration date. It is a given that we cannot share such riches without knowing and appreciating what treasures have been entrusted to our frail hands. They form part of our true identity and affect not only our thinking but also our actions, because our Catholic Faith is a living Faith. They are the patrimony given to us by God.

There are two versions of the Creed—the set of basic formulas that express our Faith as Roman Catholics. They are the *Apostles' Creed* and the *Nicene Creed*. However, in fact, these are two ancient formulas of the one and same Christian Profession of Faith. These truths cannot be altered or reformed because they belong to the Deposit of Faith. On the other hand, our understanding of them deepens due to Church teachings and the contribution of theologians faithful to the Teaching Church. In a way, it is similar to a glass: the scientist sees it as a byproduct of heating sand at extremely high temperatures, whereas a child simply sees a container for water. It still remains the same glass, the same reality, though the understanding in each instance is very different.

Our marvelous beliefs, professed in the Creed, are not some Sunday suit to be put on when we go to Church and then returned to the closet in our private homes until the following Sunday.

Christianity should not be relegated exclusively to sacred places. I believe this to be one of the major challenges to contemporary Christians. Our Faith, which contains immutable truths revealed by God Himself, is a gift from the Almighty to provide us with a mindset and a lifestyle. As is stated in the Letter to the Hebrews, "Faith is the assurance of things hoped for, the conviction of things not seen.... Without faith it is impossible to please [God]."[9] Thus, we are called to live and celebrate our Faith. Like the air inside our lungs, we must carry it wherever we go, as well as breathe it in our thoughts, words, and deeds.

The Creed is our profession of faith. It is what we confess and what we stand for as individuals and as a community during the Sunday celebration of the Holy Eucharist. But simply knowing and parroting the formulas we believe in should never be adequate. Faith is not merely a cerebral activity or verbal declaration. These formulas beckon us to enter into the implications of our Faith. By knowing our Faith better, we are able to adapt our lives to it as witnesses and to share it better with others. The next generation—indeed, all its succeeding generations—have a claim on our inheritance of God's patrimony.

Each of the two Creeds we profess is essentially divided into three parts because they proclaim our one faith in the triune God who is Father, Son, and Holy Spirit. St. Paul declared that no one can profess the Christian Creed without receiving the gift of faith from God.[10] Each article of faith contained in each Creed is like an iceberg: it declares the tip of a huge reservoir of revealed absolute truths.

---

[9]   Heb. 11:1, 6.
[10]   1 Cor. 12:3.

The Creed begins with the affirmative proclamation: "I believe in God." This might sound like a very simple statement or proclamation. But, in fact, it is a fundamental declaration that can be very deceptive in its sheer simplicity, for it is a declaration that unwraps for us an infinite world of our relationship with the Lord and with His mystery.

When we say that we believe in God, we are stating that our life adheres to God, that we welcome Jesus Christ into our personal life, and that we will live a lifestyle that shows our joyful obedience to His revelation. It is a life based and shaped by the gift of faith that we personally received from the Holy Spirit at our Baptism. Our proclamation is our intimate personal free response to the invitation from God who makes Himself known to us as individuals and as members of the Church, God's household. God gives us the gift to know and love Him as He comes to meet us and our community of faith (the Church). It is an affirmation of our personal commitment to enter into an ongoing relationship with God, who, out of sheer love, speaks to every one of us as His children[11] and intimate friends.[12] God makes Himself known to us so that, in faith and with faith, we may enter into a deep relationship with Him. As we know, dialogue is a two-way street. We speak and then we listen in our own turn.

Where can we listen to the Word of God? First of all, it is found in Sacred Scripture, the Word of God expressed in human language so that we can understand His message. This communication is carried out through faith, the phone landline, so to speak, between God and us. This spiritual phone conversation began in the Old Testament, the time of preparation for the coming of

[11] 1 John 3:1.
[12] John 15:15.

the Messiah.[13] Then, God decided, in the fullness of time,[14] to come down from Heaven and speak to us in person, in a visible and concrete way, by taking our human flesh—and the Word of God (the second Person of the Trinity) became man and dwelt among us so that, as mentioned in the Gospel of St. John, when we behold the face of Jesus, we behold the face of God.[15] But until that moment, God spoke to us as if via a landline telephone: we hear a person but do not see the speaker. The Old Testament can be considered a very long phone call made by God over many centuries. He spoke to many people, in particular to Jewish men and women of faith, as well as through events. In fact, both the Old and the New Testaments communicate the revelation of God to humanity in a variety of ways.

The whole of Sacred Scripture speaks about faith and teaches us the contents of faith by telling a story in which God unfolds His eternal plan of our salvation. As the Letter to the Hebrews teaches, "Faith is the assurance of things hoped for, the conviction of things not seen."[16] Our eyes of faith are able to see the invisible and our hearts are able to hope beyond all hope as our father in faith, Abraham, did.[17]

The Old Testament provides us with a list of outstanding persons of faith. They trusted God in moments, days, months, years, and even generations when it seemed to be foolish or meaningless to do so. They practiced the virtues of patience and perseverance and waited in vigilant hope, trust, and prayer. We should do the

---

[13]   Heb. 1:1. See also chapter 6 in this book.

[14]   Gal. 4:4–7.

[15]   John 14:9.

[16]   Heb. 11:1.

[17]   Rom. 4:18.

same as we wait with joyful hope for the return of Our Lord Jesus Christ at the end of time.

The first outstanding person of profound faith in God is Abraham. In fact, even the Church recalls and affirms this in the First Eucharistic Prayer when the priest, soon after the Words of Consecration of the bread and wine, prays, "Accept these gifts . . . as you accepted the sacrifice of Abraham, our father in faith." Abraham is the natural father from whom all Jews descend, but is also the spiritual father of all Christians. He is the first major reference point for talking about faith in God. St. Paul speaks of him as the great patriarch, the exemplary model, the father of all believers.[18] God asked Abraham to leave his country and go to a land that He would show him: "Go from your country and your kindred and your father's house to the land that I will show you."[19] It was in fact a departure from Ur of the Chaldeans into the dark, not knowing where God would lead him. It was a journey that called for radical obedience and trust, accessible only through faith. But the darkness of the unknown—the way Abraham was to go—was illuminated by the light of a promise. Though Abraham's wife, Sarah, was childless, God assured Abraham, "I will make of you a great nation, and I will bless you, and make your name great . . . and by you all the families of the earth shall bless themselves."[20] Abraham was blessed because, in faith, he knew how to discern the divine directive by surpassing appearances, trusting in God's guidance even when His ways seemed very mysterious.

What does this mean for us? When we affirm "I believe in God," we say, like Abraham: I trust You; I hand over myself to You,

---

18 Rom. 4:11-12; *Catechism of the Catholic Church*, §146.
19 Gen. 12:1.
20 Gen. 12:2-3.

Lord, but not as Someone to run to only in time of difficulty or to whom I dedicate a few moments of the day or an hour on Sundays. Saying, "I believe in God" means not only putting our life in His hands but resting there, letting His Word change us each day in our concrete choices. The prophet Jeremiah has a very poetic way of expressing this: we are like clay in a potter's hands.[21]

The second place where we find God speaking to us is in the authentic teachings of the Catholic Church. Many of us have been present at a Baptism. Remember that at a certain stage in the ceremony, we were asked three times: "Do you believe?" in God, in Jesus Christ, in the Holy Spirit, the holy Catholic Church, and the other truths of faith. Our triple response was identical: "I believe." We were also asked if we were prepared to renounce Satan and his value system. St. Ambrose commented that we should "Recall what you were asked; remember what you answered. You renounced the devil and his works, the world and its dissipation and sensuality. Your words are recorded, not on a monument to the dead but in the book of the living."[22] Our response was more than just lip service — or, at least, it ought to have been. Our personal life must go through a turning point with the gift of faith. We change and convert not from one faith to another but from one level of faith to a higher and deeper level. Perhaps, when participating at the next Baptism, we should ask ourselves how we are living out each day the gift of faith. Perhaps, we should say to the Lord what St. Paul stated in the Areopagus: in the Lord, "we live and move and have our being ... we are [your] offspring."[23]

---

[21] Jer. 18:6.
[22] St. Ambrose, *On the Mysteries*, 7.
[23] Acts 17:28.

We are visitors and outsiders on earth, for our true home is Heaven. We live in the world, but do not belong to it.[24] Faith makes us earthly pilgrims as individuals and as members of the Church and places us within the world and its history and unavoidable grave, but on the way to the heavenly homeland.[25] Believing in God makes us carriers of a value system that often does not coincide with the popular opinions of our times. Faith asks us to adopt criteria that engage us in conduct that does not belong to the worldly way of thinking and living. Christians should not be afraid to go "against the grain" in order to live our Faith. We must resist the temptation to conform, to be "one of the regular guys." This is all-important nowadays, because we are confronted with the ravages of a deadly virus and its many mutations, not to mention all this economic upheaval. Alas! God has become the "great absentee" in our society, and in His place we have erected many idols, starting with the idol known as Calling the Shots—otherwise known as *egocentricity*. We just have to look around us to see how a growing cancerous self-centeredness has created many imbalances in social behavior and in interpersonal relationships.

The good news is that the thirst for God has not vanished! The gospel message continues to resonate through the words and deeds of many people of faith. It is sometimes a difficult journey that has trials and comprises a death to worldly promises and values, but it opens onto everlasting life. It provides a major change of reality that only the eyes of faith can see and appreciate in abundance.

To say, "I believe in God" leads us to go out of ourselves continually so as to bring into our daily life the certainty that

---

[24] John 17:16.

[25] Vatican Council II, Dogmatic Constitution on the Church *Lumen Gentium* (November 21, 1964), no. 6.

comes to us from faith: God, who gives us life and salvation, is present in human history, even in today's dark moments and uncertainties. Faith in God opens us to a future with Him for a fullness of life in Heaven. Faith is always accompanied by genuine love. Neither can be hoarded; both, by their nature, demand to be shared. Thus, in sharing them, they are multiplied by those who receive them.

We should frequently remind ourselves what Pope Francis said on November 1, 2019: "We are all called to holiness."[26] He was reiterating what previous popes had pronounced since the Dogmatic Constitution on the Church of Vatican Council II of November 21, 1964.[27] Holiness is never relegated to only clergy and religious. Some laypersons might have difficulty in believing that they are called to holiness, as if there are some discarded or disqualified children of God. But this is not true, because every human being receives such a calling. On the other hand, this call to holiness does not only apply to our souls alone, but also to our bodies, which are temples of the Holy Spirit.[28] Our bodies and souls do not live in some kind of schizophrenic, dissociative relationship with one another. No: they form one person, one unit. As already stated, our Catholic Faith is a living Faith. It is not simply a proclamation parroted by our lips, but a proclamation of our mentality, lifestyle, and value system. Faith should infiltrate our very being, like a ray of light permeating a diamond and showing its inherent beauty. It is like an accent. It immediately gives us away as belonging to some other country—not the secular modernity in which we find ourselves.

---

[26] Pope Francis, Angelus, November 1, 2019.
[27] Vatican Council II, *Lumen Gentium*, nos. 39-42.
[28] 1 Cor. 6:19-20.

It is a Faith that is revealed and given by God as a mysterious free gift. Despite our personal brokenness, God has chosen each one of us by name to become His adopted child and has entrusted the awesome gift of faith to our fragile humanity, formed out of clay. We are, as St. Paul says, "earthen vessels."[29]

As we journey together across the living waters of the overflowing and refreshing river of the Catholic Faith, let our prayer be that the Holy Spirit guide us in the way of truth, based on the assurance that the Lord Jesus is "the way, and the truth, and the life; no one comes to the Father, but by me."[30]

We stand up when we declare, "I believe." The standing position is for someone who is ready to walk. Our profession of faith ends this earthly walk at the time of our death. Only then can we no longer say, "I believe," for it is at that moment that we say, "I know." This is the patrimony that God has given us!

He Is My Brother, She Is My Sister

History validates that a specific ethnic group, the Jews, has been singled out for terrible suffering at the hands of other people. Their story is full of oppression, genocide, and exile. It is a story that contains much reason for lament. Many times, the descendants of patriarch Abraham were perceived as a dying branch on the tree of humanity, withering away under the heavy weight of tyranny and persecution. Yet, at the end of each dark period, the seed of Abraham found a new spring, and the dead branch blossomed again.

Christians have also been persecuted down these two millennia since the birth of Christianity. The first people to persecute the nascent Christian Church, made up of Jewish converts, were

---

[29] 2 Cor. 4:7.
[30] John 14:6.

fellow Jews. There were many issues that led to an extraordinary tension between those Jews who became Christian and those who did not. This is mainly depicted in the Acts of the Apostles and some of the letters of St. Paul. Then came the Roman destruction of Jerusalem and the Temple and a more pronounced diaspora of all Jews, Christian converts or not, to other territories within the Roman Empire. However, providentially, this led to the growth of the Church.

Little wonder that Christians should have suffered so much — and, throughout the world, continue to suffer. Our spiritual roots are with the Jewish people. Their history is our history. This is why our Christian Scripture (the Bible) is made up of two parts: the Old and the New Testaments. What we call the Old Testament is also known as the *Hebrew Bible*. These are the Sacred Scriptures of the Jewish people. We Christians, of course, believe them to be no less sacred. But we also have the New Testament, the fulfillment and interpretation of the Hebrew Scripture in the light of God's self-revelation in the Person of Jesus Christ. The Old Testament is about the time of preparation; the New Testament is the time of the fulfillment of what had been promised and prepared for in the Old Testament. For the Christian, one Testament cannot be separated from the other. Both Testaments are like two legs that complete a person.

Each of the aforementioned two Creeds begins with the affirmation "I believe in God" and professes the revelation of the mystery of God. God made known His oneness to His Chosen People, ancient Israel. At the time, surrounding cultures believed in polytheism, where gods were ascribed and limited to a territory or function. On the other hand, unlike all of the current cultures, Israel's religion stood out because it was monotheistic. Its God was not territorial but present everywhere, He created everything, and it was impossible for God to create something bad. Everything God created was good.[31] The beautiful canticle of the prophet Daniel invites all creation to give glory to the one and true God.[32] The prophet hastened to encourage not only his fellow Jews, but the hills, the skies, the rivers, the trees, the fields, and so forth to glorify their Creator. For these, too, are the handiwork of God.

While science provides much information about the physical origins of the universe and how all life developed, Faith alone provides the correct understanding of the fact that a loving God created the universe out of nothing and that God and not chance or happenstance governs the universe.

The Church affirms that a person's mind can reach the knowledge of the existence of God on its own powers, as was the case with some ancient Greek philosophers. But this knowledge is always imprecise, for it is only through the gift of faith that we come to know the One True God. So, what did God reveal to the ancient Jews about Himself?

Israel's God is pure Spirit, while all the other gods were the product of human ingenuity or some existing object (e.g., a tree or a mountain or a river). The prophet Isaiah reminded the unfaithful Jews that the gods of other nations are not the true God: "Their land is filled with idols; they bow down to the work of their hands, to what their own fingers have made,"[33] and, "They were no gods, but the work of men's hands, wood and stone."[34] The prayer of the prophet Hezekiah[35] repeats the same thing. The divinely inspired Psalmist affirms: "Their idols are silver and gold,

---

[31] Gen. 1:31.
[32] Dan. 3:29-68.
[33] Isa. 2:8.
[34] Isa. 37:19.
[35] 2 Kings 19:14-19.

the work of men's hands."[36] There are numerous references in the Old Testament about idols.

God gave hints in the Old Testament that He is eternal and triune. This one God is Love who, in the fullness of time, fully revealed Himself: there is one God who is triune, who is Father, Son, and Holy Spirit—three Divine Persons but one God and one Lord. God is one in nature, substance, and essence. This mystery is the core of our Christian Faith and life, for it is the very mystery of God Himself. The Trinity is a mystery in the strict sense because no human mind would ever discover this unless God made Himself known and communicated to us by using imagery and language we could understand.

At the time of Moses, God was referred to as the God of Abraham, Isaac, and Jacob (renamed *Israel* by God). Then, Moses, in a very courageous moment, asked God what His name is. God responded that His divine name is *I Am Who Am*.[37] This one God revealed Himself fully in the New Testament as being triune, and the Catholic Church has sought to deepen her understanding of the Trinity from her very beginnings, fully aware that there can never be a full explanation and an exhaustive understanding of God, for God alone fully understands Himself. This should not come as a surprise to us. Let us look at ourselves: Who am I? I cannot fully understand myself. Who are you? I cannot fully understand you. Who is God? I cannot fully understand God. However, there is a big difference: we cannot fully understand ourselves and others, but God understands Himself fully. Nevertheless, God gives us hints of who He is and what He is all about, just as we give hints to one another. In this regard, we reveal ourselves,

---

[36] Ps. 115:4.
[37] Exod. 3:13–15.

making known to one another something about ourselves. God reveals Himself to us through divine revelation. The first revelation in our personal life actually takes place during the first act that was bestowed upon us as Christians: we are baptized in the name of the Trinity. Thus, from the very first moment that we become Christians, God gets involved personally in our lives as the God who is triune—Father, Son, and Holy Spirit.

Israel calls God "Father," for He is the Creator of all things seen and unseen, and of all that exists on earth and in the heavens. The language of faith draws on human parental experience when it speaks about God. Thus, God is presented in terms of human parents, both father and mother, though He is neither male nor female because He is pure spirit. God is *the Almighty* for He is universal, and nothing is impossible to Him.[38] The Lord Jesus made known the fatherhood of God by proclaiming a new understanding: God is Father by His relationship to His only Son. At the same time, the Son is Son only in relation to the Father. Jesus Christ made known the Holy Spirit, the Paraclete, who is the third Person of the Trinity. Thus, the mystery of God has been fully revealed. No one, not even the Church, can ever proclaim that there is another, a fourth, Divine Person, or one less than three Persons.

Although God could have created a perfect universe, He chose to create one that is imperfect. Sacred Scripture understands the universe to be all that exists on earth and in the heavens, assigning the earth to human beings and the heavens as the dwelling place of God and His angels, who are pure spiritual beings. Everything created, including human beings and angels, depends on the Creator for its existence.

---

[38] Matt. 19:26; Mark 10:27.

God created man and woman as His masterpiece. Angels have no bodies, and no creature but man is created in God's image. Additionally, God wanted man and woman to enter into an intimate relationship with Him. God, out of pure love, does not abandon us to our own devices, but guides and assists us through divine providence to fulfill our destiny. We are God's coworkers, but He gave us free will and always accepts our decisions, both good and bad. Because God bestowed free will to Adam and Eve, they were able to make real choices and in the process of making them they also produced their very own fully human creation: sin.

(As an aside, when people say that they are going to have a baby, they do not realize that such an act is not theirs exclusively. God must be involved in the creation of every human being. Parents are not creators of their children but co-creators with God. There are some scientists who are usurping God's creative power by artificially creating life. It is just a matter of time before nature itself revolts against this usurpation. Some scientists of our so-called advanced civilization have already begun discarding and destroying their own creations when the product is imperfect and unwanted.)

Adam and Eve were the first sinners on earth. Yet before all time and space, certain angels sinned, following Lucifer in his revolt against Heaven. Hence, the highest level of creatures, consisting of humans and angels, is responsible for introducing evil into creation. God is neither directly nor indirectly responsible for evil, for it entered the universe due to these two kinds of creatures freely choosing to sin.

God created the universe for our sake, since we occupy a very unique place in creation. Because we are made in God's image, we are the only earthly creatures who are capable of self-knowledge, real choices, self-possession, free self-giving, and interpersonal relationships with other human beings. Our vocation is to know and to love God. His grace invites us individually to enter into a divine covenant by personally responding in faith and with love.

We have to go back to basics to better know and understand ourselves and to appreciate who God really made us to be. Sacred Scripture and the Sacred Tradition of the Church teach that a person is made up of the unity of body and soul. The soul gives life to the body, which is intended to be a temple of the Holy Spirit. Parents are the means through whom their child's body is created, while God creates instantaneously at conception every human soul, which is immortal, and which will reunite with the resurrected body when time as we know it ceases to be.

Following the biblical tradition, the Catholic Church consistently teaches that the *heart* is the place where we decide to either love or reject God. God directed Adam and Eve to subdue the earth in a responsible manner.[39] He created Adam and Eve as His intimate friends, free from sensuality, greed, and egoism. This is poetically described in that passage from Genesis where God walks with them in the gentle breeze of the evening.[40] The couple

---

[39] Pope Francis, in an address to members of the European Parliament in Strasbourg on November 24, 2014, referred to our relationship with nature: "Each of us has a personal responsibility to care for creation, this precious gift which God has entrusted to us. This means, on the one hand, that nature is at our disposal so as to enjoy and use properly. Yet it also means that we are not its masters. We are stewards, but not masters. We need to love and respect nature. Instead we are often guided by the pride of dominating, possessing, manipulating, exploiting. We do not 'preserve' the Earth, we do not respect it, we do not consider it as a freely given gift to look after. Respect for the environment, however, means more than not destroying it; it also means using it for good purposes."

[40] This is implied in Gen. 3:8.

was to live in harmony with God and all He had created. That is why Eden was called a Paradise. But our first parents frustrated God's plan by committing the first sin, thus staining human nature with Original Sin. Their free will allowed them to make the first wrong choice, and wrong choices have been made ever since. They disobeyed God. We are very familiar with the scene when Satan, appearing as an alluring serpent, seduced and deceived them. They believed that they would become gods.[41] It is rather ironic that this was a duplication of the sin of Lucifer (Satan): he wanted to be a god![42] The original harmony was shattered, and Adam and Eve began a struggle that all of us also experience: we struggle within ourselves, among ourselves, and with nature. Once sin entered humanity, it was there to stay.

Pope Francis has frequently stated that sin is real, concrete, and always present in human history, despite avid attempts to ignore it, excuse it, or present it as some flaw for which a person lacks responsibility. Today's society seems to think that something immoral or criminal is fine as long as one is not caught. It is something like going over the speed limit. It is fine until one gets a speeding ticket. Then it becomes bad. Or shoplifting is fine until one gets caught and gets into trouble with the law. Sin is unmasked by appreciating the profound relationship between a person and God, because sin in one way or another is a free rejection of God.

All time belongs to God, and this should leave no place for sin in our human time. Divine revelation crystallizes the reality of sin. The knowledge of God's plan for humanity enables us to grasp the true reality of sin and its very real consequences. Original Sin infected the entire human race through human nature, rendering

[41] Gen. 3:5.
[42] Isa. 14:12–17.

every person in need of salvation through Christ. The result was the punishment of death and the loss of grace by the first parents and all of their descendants (except for Mary and Jesus) through human nature itself.

Some might claim that it is unfair, that we are being penalized for someone else's sin. However, even our natural behavior indicates that sometimes we are negatively affected by another person. Let us say that we are on the highway and the car in front of us stalls. What happens? All the cars behind it come to a stop. All drivers are affected by something they did not do. In a way, one might say that Adam and Eve were the first car to stall. This stalling is Original Sin. Now all the drivers behind them—you, and me, and every other human being who has ever lived and ever will live—are affected by it.

We are all wounded by our enemy—sin. The Divine Doctor heals us, but all of us walk with a spiritual limp, a spiritual weakness, for we remain prone to sin.

The Catholic Church teaches that the Sacrament of Baptism erases the stain of Original Sin and sins committed prior to one's reception of the sacrament.[43] However, the Sacrament of Baptism does not take away the weakened state of our human nature. We have a spiritual battle for the rest of our lives on earth. Personal sin, my sinning, is my free decision to reject God in that I want to do my own thing regardless of what God wants of me.

Satan has never given up on his war against God. Satan constantly tries to induce us to sin. That is why God sent His only Son to destroy this power of Satan. Christ, by suffering and dying and rising from the dead, restored humanity to God's friendship and set it free from the grip of Satan. The Sacrament of Baptism enables

---

[43] CCC, §1263. See also chapter 17.

us to become members of the household of God. As members of this household, you are my sister, you are my brother.

Shepherd and Walker

There are times in Sacred Scripture when Jesus is presented to us as a Shepherd[44] and other times when He is presented as a Walker.[45] This dual role reaches back to the Old Testament imagery.[46]

The two Books of Chronicles span some 550 years of the history of the Jewish people, starting with the death of Saul, their first king, around 1010 BC, down to the return of the Jews from the Babylonian Exile, beginning in 539 BC. The original parents of these people, as is the case with us, are identified in the book of Genesis—Adam and Eve—but the sources of their Jewish race are the great patriarch Abraham and his wife Sarah, chosen by God to be the parents of numberless descendants.[47] They formed the elected People of God, the Jewish people. These were usually very rebellious, counterfeiting their allegiance to an all-knowing and most loving Father. But God was madly in love with His chosen people.[48] Many a time He closed His eyes to their idolatrous, unfaithful, and distrusting behavior. They had to be brought back into line over and over again. God did so by loosening their ties with their God-given land and allowing them to be taken to a foreign country—Babylon, a place alien both to Jews and their God—and there be purified of their sinfulness. Then, God acts like the first role: like a shepherd, God goes to

---

44 Matt. 2:6, 9:36, 26:31; Mark 6:34, 14:27; John 10:11, 14; Heb. 13:30; 1 Pet. 5:4.

45 John 1:14; Heb. 4:15.

46 2 Chron. 36:14–16, 19–23; Ps. 137:1–2, 6.

47 Gen. 22:17.

48 Deut. 7:7–8.

recover the lost sheep and carries it on His shoulders, bringing it back to His land of promise where the sheep will be nurtured, nourished, and safe. This is revealed in the sacred history found in Second Chronicles.

The second role is the Walker. A walker needs walking shoes. The profession and talent of a cobbler is practically lost in the States. The great majority of shoes are factory-made. But a cobbler is a real artist and goes to great lengths to produce shoes. He measures each foot; he pencils around each foot, considering the unique way our foot is shaped, and so forth. In other words, he wants to produce a pair of shoes that is a perfect fit. God the Father does this through the Old Testament teachings presented by prophets and saintly women and men. Then, when the shoes are produced in the fullness of time, God fits them into the feet of His divine Son and sends Him to walk the earth—to walk among us as one of us, His rebellious children. Jesus walks our walk, covers the same terrain that our feet cover, and lights up the path that has been darkened by sin, including our sins. This Walker and the Shepherd are one and the same in Jesus Christ.

Pope Francis has urged bishops and priests to acquire the "smell of the fold of the sheep" entrusted to them.[49] If you have been around sheep, they have a very distinct and repulsive smell. What does the Holy Father mean? I think he wants us—the clergy—to suffer with our flocks. He wants us to be immersed in their suffering, anxiety, fear, heartache, disillusionment, and broken promises. We should not be bystanders in our children's lives. Rather, we

---

[49] Pope Francis, Homily at the Chrism Mass on Holy Thursday, St. Peter's Basilica (March 28, 2013); Pope Francis, Apostolic Exhortation on the Proclamation of the Gospel in Today's World *Evangelii Gaudium* (November 24, 2013), no. 24.

should feel the burden of such sufferings. We should walk their walk, as Christ does.

And I would venture to say that this does not only apply to bishops and priests but to all Christians.[50] We all owe our neighbors a duty of service, compassion, and forgiveness. St. John Chrysostom reminded his contemporaries that "as long as we are sheep, we overcome and, though surrounded by countless wolves, we emerge victorious."[51] All of us are challenged to do so today, especially during this dark time of the long reign of Covid-19 and its aftermath, including the worldwide economic crisis. St. Paul reminds us in the Letter to the Ephesians that the source of our fraternal service is through practicing the gift of faith that our Heavenly Father has freely bestowed upon each and every one of us, His beloved children.[52]

Like the Jews in Second Chronicles, we sin by disguising our selfish love as something godly. We exchange Christian values for the dazzling allurements of the world. We doubt our Heavenly Father's love and care for His children. But we are reminded that Jesus is the Good Shepherd who seeks us out to pick us up, place us on His shoulders,[53] and bring us back to the sacred land of God, the sanctuary of God where Jesus is fully present in the Holy Eucharist. Then we are forgiven, nourished, nurtured, and bonded with our brothers and sisters as members of Mother Church and hear His words: do not be afraid, for I am with you always until the end of time.[54]

---

[50] Pope Francis, Address to Officials and Staff of the *Aggiornamenti Sociali* Magazine, (December 6, 2019).

[51] St. John Chrysostom, *Homily on Matthew*, homily 33, 1.

[52] Eph. 1:4-10.

[53] Luke 15:1-7.

[54] Matt. 28:20.

We are encouraged by hearing the words that came from the depth of the Immaculate Heart of the Mother of God as she carried God's Son in her virginal womb: "He has helped his servant Israel, in remembrance of his mercy, as he spoke to our fathers, to Abraham and to his posterity for ever."[55] Our Lady's words were echoed by the "unmuted" Zachariah, the father of John the Baptist: "[He promised] to perform the mercy promised to our fathers, and to remember his holy covenant.... in the forgiveness of their sins."[56] This is the fountain that gives us reason to rejoice—*gaudete et laetare*. This is what makes us Catholics unique: the Word of God and the Holy Eucharist.

---

[55] Luke 1:54-55.
[56] Luke 1:72, 77.

2

Spending Time

Time Is a Messenger of God

Our present world is surrounded by all kinds of turmoil. It is difficult to imagine that much of it usually traces its roots back to the disorder in our own personal life. The turmoil that we experience as clergy or parents or siblings or employers or employees is usually similar to those of many other individuals, though we might think that ours is unique. When this turmoil is added together with those of others, they infiltrate the life of a nation's community, as well as the world of economics, and penetrate into both the family as a nation and the domain of business. On the other hand, there is also spiritual turmoil. The value system of the world competes with the Christian moral system and tries to silence it by attempting to usurp its place in the life of Christian believers. We end up with much confusion when many of our decisions are not illuminated by the light of Christ. Consequently, our souls find themselves in turmoil. But for those who are faithful to the Lord, the search for inner stillness goes on in the midst of personal, national, and international upheaval, and, with St. Augustine, they cry out to the Lord: "You have made us for Yourself, O Lord, and our heart is restless until it rests in You."[57]

There are instances when we hear or read something and we begin to feel uncomfortable with some aspect of our own selves. In general, confrontations with others are very difficult, but a confrontation with oneself is considerably more difficult. We must be convinced that the Lord raises His hand to touch, heal, and strengthen us with His abiding grace. One can compare it to some sort of a spiritual surgery being carried out by our Divine Doctor and Healer. As is the case following a physical surgery, we first feel the pain, then we gently sit up in bed, then we take the first painful steps with the help of others. Next, we might be given a walker to steady our movement, and finally we gain complete independence and move around as the pain becomes more bearable and begins to dissipate. When it comes to spiritual surgery, we are both patient and assisting surgeon!

But we do not do surgery on our own. Rather, we are being guided by the teachings of the Lord and His Church, strengthened by God's grace and illumined by the Holy Spirit to pin down the real sickness, the spiritual tumor called sin. This kind of surgery undergoes a number of steps. First, we make the Sign of the Cross and ask the Lord for assistance. Second, we make an honest—and many times painful—examination of our conscience. Third, we take the scalpel of God's truth to make the first painful incision. Fourth, using the Ten Commandments, we identify our spiritual tumors (our sins). Fifth, we ask God to heal us—to forgive us—and help us turn our lives over to the Divine Doctor to have the tumors removed through the Sacrament of Confession. Sixth, we try to change our lives by first moving slowly and up to complete

[57] St. Augustine, *Confessions*, bk. 1:2.

movement, brought about and sustained through the grace of God, prayer, and self-discipline.

It is a proven fact by disinterested sources that the most persecuted body of believers in the world today is Christians. I think we should not be surprised with reading, hearing, or watching on the news the presence of persecution of Christians. This outside turmoil, inflicted by non-believers in the Lord, is part and parcel of the history of Christianity, something that goes back to the very beginning of the Church. We should recall that the Acts of the Apostles speaks of the persecution of the apostles who preached the name of Jesus on the day of Pentecost.[58] The persecution of the Church began soon after the Lord's Resurrection. The apostles were thrown into one of the prisons in Jerusalem for preaching the good news. Then an angel of the Lord set them free, only for them to be brought once again before the Jewish Court composed of very learned men, the Sanhedrin. Next, we have the first martyrdom in the Church: the deacon Stephen is stoned to death, with a young man called Saul (later known as St. Paul) standing by and approving of the execution.[59]

Christians should not be surprised by the turmoil of persecution. It is rooted in the public ministry of Jesus. Though He is the long-awaited Messiah, He came to what was His own and His own people rejected Him.[60] The people the Lord loved not only rejected Him, but many of them were the religious and political leaders of Israel. The Pharisees, the Sadducees, and the Herodians conspired together to bring about His death as a criminal. Yet, the Lord remained internally still amidst this external turmoil, for He

[58] Acts 5:34–42.
[59] Acts 7:54–8:1.
[60] John 1:11.

came to do the will of His Heavenly Father.[61] He exhorted His twelve apostles to not let their hearts be troubled,[62] in other words, to let their hearts be still. What happened in the lives of the first Christians and what is happening today in our contemporary world is a duplication of what happened to the Lord, and He invites us to be internally still amidst this external turmoil.

Who were the people that judged the apostles and persecuted them and the other members of the nascent Christian community, and for what reason? They belonged to the Sanhedrin and, it is reasonable to assume, were the same persons who defamed and condemned Jesus for a couple of months before His trial. Many members of the Sanhedrin belonged to the upper class in Jewish society and were prominent intellectuals. Many of them were very learned and doctors in Jewish Law and interpreted to the Jewish population the precepts of the Mosaic Law. They could not tolerate the proclamation of the Person or the message of Jesus Christ. They felt that their job and authority were being threatened. They decided that these illiterate Galilean preachers and their followers had to be stopped at all costs. The Sanhedrin had the power to condemn to death, though they could not carry out any capital punishment without the approval of the Roman authorities. This was the case with the Lord's Crucifixion.

However, we must also recall that not all the members of the Sanhedrin were bad news. There was Nicodemus, a good man though a secret follower of Jesus.[63] There was the very prudent and just Gamaliel,[64] who stood up before the Sanhedrin and advised

---

[61] Mark 14:36; Luke 22:42.
[62] John 14:1.
[63] John 3:2.
[64] Acts 5:34–39.

great caution when dealing with the accused apostles. Gamaliel was a person of moral authority, someone who could not be easily dismissed or ignored. He saved the apostles. He advised that during this time, many came forward claiming to be the Messiah and were proven counterfeit. He also stated that if these Galilean men have been sent by God, the members of the Sanhedrin ran the risk of going against God. He recommended that the apostles should be given a grave warning and then let go, for it was just a matter of time before they proved whether they were authentic messengers of God or not. And this is exactly what happened.

How many of us are good but follow Christ secretly, as if we are mortified to be known as Christians? We may see ourselves as following Jesus by upholding Christian values, but even a non-baptized person can uphold Christian values without becoming Catholic, as was the case with figures like Mahatma Gandhi. Why? Because an authentic Catholic does not only live by Christian values. By virtue of his Baptism, he is a missionary. He should proclaim the Lord, should identify himself as a Christian. He should resist the values of the world replacing Christian values. Our beliefs are similar to a water fountain; its waters flow and become a source to quench the thirst of those who are looking for Jesus to provide them with stillness of the heart.

Let us reflect for a moment on the dynamics of what happened at the above indicated trial of the apostles in front of the Sanhedrin, for there are also many voices in our society that claim to have a message from God, a new approach to Jesus, a new way of living as a Christian, and they go ahead and condemn Catholics. There are also times when even Catholics condemn the Church, the pope, bishops and priests, religious, and their fellow Catholics. They claim to possess a special message. But can this be true? Can it be that the Church, which Christ assured is guided by the Holy Spirit down the ages and until He returns in glory, has been misleading people of good will for two thousand years? Many persons during these two thousand years have come forward with their own versions of Christianity, their own versions of Christian morality and values, and their own versions of Christian living. The Catholic Church is the only one that has survived turbulent times since her foundation two thousand years ago. The others may have flourished for a while, may have been temporarily successful, may have gathered plenty of followers, but in the end they either disappeared or became divided and splintered, scattered like leaves blown away by the wind.

Perhaps some of us have come up with our personal versions of what it means to be a Christian and uphold a moral code that does not completely embrace the moral teachings of the Catholic Faith. In other words, we do not match the Lord's blueprint. Perhaps we should learn something from Gamaliel: with patience, time will tell.

It is interesting that the words of Gamaliel have had a long-lasting effect on the growth of the Catholic Faith. By advising his colleagues to be patient and allow time to run its course, the small number of Christians at that time were spared extinction. The message of Christ spread and the Church grew. The brilliant minds of some of the members of the Sanhedrin, of the men who would not tolerate anyone else who had a different interpretation of the Hebrew Scriptures, of the people who did not understand dialogue and expected others to do what they were told, accepted Gamaliel's advice to be patient and take time. Why? Because taking time leaves room for hope, and on many occasions, time is the messenger of God. It seems that Gamaliel's recommendation also applies to us today.

The English poet John Donne wrote that "no man is an island." In other words, we are social by nature and we must relate to others. Sometimes, these relationships go sour. Thus, when we feel or think something bad against another person—a spouse, a parent, a sibling, an in-law, an employer, or a fellow employee—and we do not seek resolution, tension within us and between us grows and finally it explodes into gossip, sarcasm, lies, hate, and so many other harmful things. We might justify ourselves by claiming that we are deeply hurt or cheated. Thus, bad feelings become more ingrained and make us indifferent to the well-being of the other person. We continue to justify our unvirtuous way of dealing with such a person.

We should remember that it takes a very short time to do an evil thing and that time passes but the evil remains. For example, when we enter into a very serious fight with a family member or any other person, the actual exchange of nasty words takes up very little time, but the bad effects remain for hours or days or weeks or, even in some cases, years. Gamaliel offers us the correct medicine for such things: stop your feelings from controlling you and give yourself time to reflect, recover, and heal.

As is the case with committing an evil act, a virtuous act is short in duration, but its good effects remain. Time has its own way of putting things in harmony and showing us what is right. There is one sure thing: if we react in a moment of anger or deep hurt, we will surely be unjust. However, being unjust does not only harm the other person, but it also harms us, for if we do not step back from the situation, the bad feelings and thoughts within us grow like weeds and get deeper until they explode in hostility and hatred. We build up our own prisons by our unchristian emotions and imagination. When we have evil thoughts and bad feelings against others, we are struggling against God, because God loves the others, God loves harmony, God loves peace, God loves dialogue, God loves walking together with us.

St. Paul reminds us: "Blessed be the God and Father of our Lord Jesus Christ, the Father of mercies and God of all comfort, who comforts us in all our affliction."[65] On the other hand, when we feel hurt or angry we usually do not think of God first, but rather we think of getting even or hurting the one who hurt us by retaliating. We become absorbed in egocentricity. Surely, such a thing is not from God. So, we have to stop, step back, and take time to allow room for the Holy Spirit, so He may slowly heal us and lead us to what is just, to peace. We are to be patient and trusting, for, as the inspired Psalmist declared centuries ago: "Out of my distress I called on the LORD; the LORD answered me and set me free. With the LORD on my side I do not fear. What can man do to me? The LORD is at my side to help me.... It is better to take refuge in the LORD than to put confidence in man. It is better to take refuge in the LORD than to put confidence in princes."[66] Time is a messenger of God.

Things That Really Matter

It seems that one of the best ways to attract almost instantaneously a huge Catholic crowd, even those whose body has not shadowed the door of a church for decades, is to say that there was a miracle, such as a statue bleeding, or Our Lady appearing somewhere.

Yet, when the greatest miracle of all takes place, and its truth is assured by the Lord Jesus Himself, there is no big crowd rushing to a church, as tragically the ongoing Pew Research Center surveys inform us. In fact, many people complain of how boring or non-stimulating it is!

I am referring to the miracle of the Holy Eucharist. Every time that a priest, whether he is a great sinner or saint, consecrates the bread and wine, these elements become Jesus Christ Himself.

---

[65] 2 Cor. 1:3-5.
[66] Ps. 118: 5-9.

The Father sent His Eternal Son not by some chance or by a decision on the spur of the moment or by an afterthought, but at the fullness of time.[67] He came not as a messenger, as happened with the prophets of old, but as the Teacher. As St. John declares: "God so loved the world that he gave his only Son."[68] The same is revealed in the Letter to the Hebrews:

> In many and various ways God spoke of old to our fathers by the prophets; but in these last days he has spoken to us by a Son, whom he appointed the heir of all things, through whom also he created the world. He reflects the glory of God and bears the very stamp of his nature, upholding the universe by his word of power. When he had made purification for sins, he sat down at the right hand of the Majesty on high, having become as much superior to angels as the name he has obtained is more excellent than theirs.[69]

I suspect that one of the main reasons for our failure to appreciate the silent miracle of the Holy Eucharist lies in the fact that we are sensory people. We want to see, touch, taste, smell, and hear. We cannot physically see or touch the miracle of the Most Holy Eucharist, but we can see and touch a bleeding statue or see and hear Our Lady appearing in a vision. I would venture to say that it is similar to the miracle of our conception: when God creates us individually through the cooperation of our parents, human life is created in silence. It is a miracle, yet it is very real and concrete.

When there is a true miracle or an authentic vision, there is also an encounter with God. When this happens, the believing

---

[67] Gal. 4:4.
[68] John 3:16.
[69] Heb. 1:1–4.

Christian must resist the temptation of going from the wonder of encountering the Lord to trying to exploit it, thereby giving in to the spirit of worldliness and becoming contaminated. I have given a couple of retreats in Fátima and have been to Lourdes a number of times. It is very disheartening to see so much mundane business going on around each site. People open shops. Others sell cheap trinkets in the streets. Food is very expensive. Many, though not all, of the people who run such businesses do not care about how much it costs a pilgrim physically and financially. Rather, it is business as usual. The scene reminds me of Jesus on the way to the Cross. Here is the wonderful event of our redemption taking place, but people looked outside the shop and saw a beaten man carrying a cross, made some nasty remark because they thought He was a criminal, and then went back to their business. They had no clue that what was actually happening a few yards away from them was their redemption! These people were involved in things that mattered to them right then and there and not things that matter for all eternity. In other words, they were too busy with things of earth, mindless of the things of Heaven. We cannot simply dismiss them or condemn them, for many a time we are very similar to such people. We are in church for Holy Mass, but our minds are miles away—thinking of problems at work or in the family, worrying about some dish we left cooking in the oven, and so forth. There are some who are distracted even while lining up to receive Holy Communion, busy shaking hands with other people in the line and whispering greetings as they approach to receive Holy Communion. Some are so distracted that they open their mouth to stick out their tongue and present their hands simultaneously to receive Holy Communion. When we do these things, we are not in tune with the miracle of the Holy Eucharist. We forget that Jesus is present in His fullness just for our personal sake!

There is a magnificent scene in the Gospel of St. John that depicts the miracle of the Multiplication of the Loaves.[70] Scripture scholars and theologians see in this miracle an anticipation of Holy Eucharist. Many of those five thousand men—not counting women and children—followed the Lord after He performed this miracle. What is interesting here is that perhaps the real reason why they went to seek Jesus was very practical. They did not ask: What does this really mean? Instead, they asked: Will He do this every day? Can I quit my job and live off of His magic fish and loaves?

What mattered to them was the physical, concrete, and practical. They were interested in what Jesus could give them in material things and not in what He was trying to teach them in things that matter. Therefore, when Jesus began to speak about Himself as the Bread come down from Heaven, that He is the Bread of Life, that He will give them His flesh to eat, even some of His disciples, some of His close followers, found this very hard to accept and abandoned Him.[71]

Let us reflect for a moment on the issue of nourishment. The Synoptic Gospels relate how Jesus went to the desert before He began His preaching and teaching, that is His public ministry of the proclamation of the good news.[72] All of us are familiar with this episode. While in the desert for forty days and nights, Jesus denied Himself physical food. He fasted and prayed. At the end of the forty days—which symbolized the forty days that Moses spent on Mount Sinai (Horeb) before God gave him the Ten Commandments and the forty years that the Hebrew slaves spent wandering in the Sinai Desert before reaching the Promised Land—Jesus was tempted.

---

[70] John 6:1-15.
[71] John 6:25-66.
[72] Matt. 4:1-11; Mark 1:12-13; Luke 4:1-13.

The first temptation[73] was about physical nourishment: turn these stones into bread. Jesus responds by saying that man does not live by bread alone, but by every word that comes from the mouth of God. When we go beyond the material and take into account the spiritual, we set things in their right perspective. In other words, many a time we spend a lot of time, energy, and money in getting what we want rather than in getting what we need for both body and soul. In order for us to realize what we truly need, we must allow God to enter into the picture. Then we realize the things that really matter. And this is why the Gospels inform us that Jesus was filled with the power of the Spirit.

We are then told that Jesus left the desert and went to preach to people of what things really matter. He went to Nazareth, where He grew up, and there He announced His mission with the passage from the Prophet Isaiah: "The Spirit of the Lord is upon me, because he has anointed me to preach good news to the poor. He has sent me to proclaim release to the captives and recovering of sight to the blind, to set at liberty those who are oppressed, and to proclaim the acceptable year of the Lord."[74] This was Jesus' mission. Once He proclaimed His mission, then began the miracles, the signs, the healings, and His teaching.

The people to whom He preached were practical. They saw these healings and believed in Him and brought the sick to Him to heal them. But Jesus wasn't just trying to save them money on their medical bills. He performed miracles because it was part of His mission. He addressed their physical and material needs, then used the occasion to teach them through His parables. He fed their bodies, then their souls.

---

[73]   Matt. 4:3; Luke 4:3.
[74]   Luke 4:14–21.

Most of his listeners, however, did not get it. They loved what they saw (sick people restored to health), what they tasted (the multiplied bread and fish), and only to the extent that they had these physical and material needs met were they willing to listen to His teaching, which they deemed to be extraordinary, delivered with authority, and impressive.[75] But they were stuck on material things. They couldn't see past the miracles. They spoke of Him as a prophet, a man of God. They wanted to exploit Jesus and take advantage of Him, and wanted to make Him king![76] When they did not see Him the following morning, them went to look for Him. But they held on to Jesus only insofar as their physical needs were met.

Are we not the same way? Is it not usual that we go to places where we can see with our own eyes the results of miracles? Is it not easier for us to be good Catholics as long as Jesus answers our prayers according to our expectations? We want to touch, to see, to smell, to taste, to hear and experience the answer to our prayers. But the miracle of the Holy Eucharist, the full and Real Presence of Jesus Christ, is not seen or touched or smelled or heard or tasted. Hence, we miss the greatest miracle of all in our lives! We forget that beautiful prayer of St. Teresa of Ávila: "Let nothing disturb you, let nothing dismay you. All things pass away. God never changes. Patience attains all that it strives for. He who has God finds he lacks nothing. God alone suffices."[77] Alas, many a time, we miss the things that really matter.

We are allured by power. This is the jest of the second temptation of Jesus.[78] Satan promised to give Jesus all earthly power

---

[75] Matt. 7:28–29; Luke 4:31–32.

[76] John 6:15.

[77] Known as the bookmark of St. Teresa of Ávila (1515–1582).

[78] Matt. 4:5–6; Luke 4:5–7.

(something that was not Satan's to give!) if Jesus would worship him. Would we be able to withstand such a promise? Might we not want to be in command and in control? We so often yearn to have people at our beck and call. We would like to have people immediately follow our directives and wishes. We might want to make choices for people, irrespective of what they think. We might want to spread our weight around at home, at work, in the parish community, in society in general, and threaten repercussions if our demands go unheeded. We might expect some important position or special treatment at the parish due to our generous offerings. In other words, we aim at establishing our little kingdom. Jesus, on the other hand, teaches us that our vocation is to be servants called to establish the Kingdom of God on earth. Earthly power makes us vain; heavenly power makes us saints. These are things that really matter.

We are also attracted by some kind of spectacle. This is also found in the third temptation of Jesus at the end of His forty-day fast in the desert.[79] The devil takes Jesus to the top of the Temple of Jerusalem where people in the area can see Him. Then he tells Jesus: jump! People will notice You and because no harm will come to You, then they will believe in You, and consider how holy and good You are, because You will not be hurt; they will become convinced that You are special to God, for God offers You His protection. In other words, make a fine display of Yourself, and be noticed. Impress people. Show off.

Jesus, in a way, alludes to this when He speaks to those who followed Him after the miracle of the Multiplication of the Loaves. He did not turn stones into bread, as the devil requested, but He made five loaves feed five thousand. Jesus, ever realistic, told those

---

[79] Matt. 4:8–9; Luke 4:9.

who benefitted from the miracle: "Truly, truly I say to you, you seek me, not because you saw signs, but because you ate your fill of the loaves."[80]

It seems that some people go to Holy Mass without having a basic notion of what it is all about, and expect to be treated the same way they are treated when they go, for example, to a play or the movies or some show. Hence, they feel somewhat disappointed when they do not leave self-satisfied. But we should go to Holy Mass to have a direct audience with God and with the worshipping community, with our Christian brothers and sisters. We have an audience with God in person, for Jesus comes down from Heaven at the Words of Consecration. He is truly and fully present. Thus, we should listen to the Eucharistic Prayer that the priest prays and that we witness and, hopefully, join in by praying and paying attention. Each Eucharistic Prayer is very interesting and a catechesis in itself. Let us look at the beginning of Eucharistic Prayer 2:

> You are indeed Holy, O Lord, the fount of all holiness. Make holy, therefore, these gifts, we pray, by sending down Your Spirit upon them like the dewfall, so that they may become for us the Body and Blood of our Lord Jesus Christ. At the time He was betrayed and entered willingly into His Passion, He took bread and, giving thanks, broke it, and gave it to His disciples, saying: Take this all of you, and eat it for *This is My Body, which will be given up for you.* In a similar way, when supper was ended, He took the chalice and, once more giving thanks, He gave it to His disciples, saying: take this, all of you, and drink from it, for *This is the chalice of My Blood, the Blood of the new and eternal covenant,*

which will be poured out for you and for many for the forgiveness of sins. Do this in memory of Me.

Then the priest declares the mystery of faith and the worshipping community acclaims that when they eat the bread and drink the wine, they proclaim the Lord's death until His return in glory at the end of time.

God, accompanied by His angels and saints, comes down from Heaven during the celebration of Holy Mass. But there is no visible spectacle! We do not see some blinding light, we do not hear angels singing, we do not hear the saints' voices praising God. All is done in silence, but all is real, all is true. God, in His love and mercy for the unworthy priest and the rest of us, all sinners and undeserving, comes down from Heaven to be with us. When we go to Holy Mass out of habit or mindlessness or because we feel we have to do so for otherwise we sin, we miss the things that really matter: God's love and mercy toward us and God's way of being among us fully present. Such things really matter.

Time with the Eucharistic Jesus Changes Us

There seems to be something that does not fit in well when it comes to the celebration of Holy Mass. I invite you to ask yourself: why is it that for some people Holy Mass seems to be more true, more holy, when an important member of the clergy celebrates it, as if it is not the same Lord who comes down from Heaven? Up to the outbreak of Covid-19, I received regular requests from people to help them attend one of the early morning Holy Masses celebrated by Pope Francis at Casa Santa Marta, where he resides. There were times when I wondered if such requests were based on one's considering oneself as more worthy than the rest of us. However, we priests are not the true source of Holy Mass. Rather, Christ is—the one Christ who is equally present at every Mass, no matter who is the celebrant. In other words, these privileges and graces come from Christ and not from the priest celebrant. Of course, there is nothing wrong with asking for such a Mass, but we have to examine the reason behind our request.

Mistakenly, there are some whose participating at Holy Mass seems to be attached to some emotional issue on their part. Perhaps this seems to be the case with most of us! We seem to be more fervent and joyful at a pope's or bishop's Holy Mass than at the one on Sunday in our parish. Yet are two different Christs present? Do we tend to focus on the one who celebrates Mass rather than on the God who comes down from Heaven under the appearances of bread and wine?

We have to keep in mind the humility and the mercy of God, who binds Himself to the Words of Consecration, irrespective of the holiness or sinfulness of the one who is celebrant. The same Jesus becomes fully present at a Holy Mass celebrated by the greatest saint and by the most corrupt priest. Pope Francis once said:

> *In the Eucharist fragility is strength:* the strength of the love that becomes small so it can be welcomed and not feared; the strength of the love that is broken and shared so as to nourish and give life; the strength of the love that is split apart so as to join all of us in unity ... the strength to love those who make mistakes.... And above all he heals us from those fragilities that we cannot heal on our own, with love.... That of feeling resentment toward those who have done us harm ... that of distancing ourselves from others and closing off within ourselves ... that of feeling sorry for ourselves and complaining without finding peace.

He went on to say that the Lord "gives us the courage to go outside of ourselves and bend down with love toward the fragility of others. As God does with us. This is the logic of the Eucharist: we receive Jesus who loves us and heals our fragilities in order to love others and help them in their fragilities."[81] The bottom line is that what really matters is that we are in the presence of Christ and being nourished by Him. Our emotions, our feelings, are secondary at best.

When we do not concentrate on Jesus, especially His full and Real Presence in Holy Eucharist,[82] we run the great risk of becoming Christian in name only, having an external attitude as a detached spectator, for our heart lies elsewhere. We are performing a pious act, not a *holy* act. St. Peter tells us how we ought to behave in a concrete way: "For this very reason make every effort to supplement your faith with virtue, and virtue with knowledge, and knowledge with self-control, and self-control with steadfastness, and steadfastness with godliness, and godliness with brotherly affection, and brotherly affection with love."[83] Faith gives birth to concrete love.

We must fall in love with the living Jesus. Otherwise we will be like those who followed Him after the miracle of the multiplication of the loaves, and He will tell us the same words He told them: "Truly, truly, I say to you, you seek me, not because you saw signs, but because you ate your fill of the loaves."[84] In our case, it would be tied to the way our prayers, wishes, and emotions are met by God. Herein lies our daily temptation: slipping toward worldliness

---

[81] Pope Francis, Angelus (June 6, 2021).
[82] CCC, §§1374–1377.
[83] 2 Pet. 1:5–7.
[84] John 6:26.

because we follow Jesus when He pleases us, when we feel the power of our prayer, and hence, when we do this, our mission to proclaim the real Lord weakens.

It seems that some of the people who had been fed at the miracle of the multiplication of the loaves understood Jesus' rebuke, for they asked Him: "What must we do, to be doing the works of God?" Jesus answered them: "This is the work of God, that you believe in him whom he has sent."[85]

In other words, to have faith in Christ, in Jesus alone; to trust in Christ and not in other things that eventually lead us far away from Jesus, such as when a favorite priest is transferred and then we stop going to Church. We should always keep in mind that the priest-servant who is sent is not greater than the one who sent him, and is not greater than his Master, Jesus the High Priest. Let us implore that every prayer, especially the prayer of Holy Mass, be an astonishment of our encounter with Jesus, for He helps us not to fall into the spirit of worldliness, which is the spirit that is behind or under a superficial layer of Christianity that will lead us to live as pagans who simply live our spiritual life through gestures and not by our conviction in the Lord. Pious acts have their proper place, but holiness is the aim.

Each of us is called to have a personal encounter with the Lord, a true and actual encounter that can radically change our lives. We can have a very long relationship with someone over the phone, Facebook, WhatsApp, and so forth. We know them somewhat, though we have yet to meet them. However, once we meet them, our interpersonal dynamics change drastically. I think the same can be said about our relationship with the Lord. The secret lies not only in being aware of the encounter, but also in

---

[85] John 6:28-29.

never forgetting it, so as to preserve its freshness and beauty. We can look at the life of St. Paul to see how he remembered, how his life was radically changed, once he encountered the Lord Jesus on his way to Damascus to arrest Christians, as narrated in the Acts of the Apostles.[86] He originally carried the name of *Saul*, which meant in Hebrew "asked or prayed for." His new name was *Paul*, meaning in Hebrew, "humble" or "small."

Saul was absolutely certain of the teachings of the Hebrew Scripture he had received in his childhood and youth. He was very zealous about imposing this on others, in particular those Jews who had become Christians. Unity in the true faith of the Hebrews was extremely important to Saul. He saw Jewish Christians shattering that unity among God's Chosen People. His zeal led him to persecute Jewish members of the nascent Christian sect. Thus, Saul asked for letters that he would present to the synagogues at Damascus, authorizing him to put Christians in chains. He carried out this mission with the same zeal for God of the prophet Elijah.[87]

But all of us know what happened to Saul on his way to Damascus. He had a vision, and fell off the horse. At that point the Lord spoke to him: "Saul, Saul, why do you persecute me?" "Who are you, Lord?" asks Saul. "I am Jesus."[88] Until the moment of his encounter with Jesus, Saul believed that everything said by Christians was mere fiction. But here he encountered Christ Himself. So, he defected. St. Paul spent the rest of his life proclaiming Jesus to the world as the means of salvation. He fell off his high horse of righteousness, of being more zealous than the rest of the people, of being more holy than they, of being more learned than they,

---

[86] Acts 9:1–20.
[87] 1 Kings 19:10.
[88] Acts 9:4–5; 26:14–15.

of his rigidity, and of claiming to be closer to God than most. He realized that his great convictions were misplaced.

The Bible recounts many Old Testament encounters with God, as well as encounters with Jesus in the Gospels. They are all different, as different as there are men and women, but as true and real as each one had his or her own encounter with Jesus. Let us think about the two first disciples who followed Jesus, as the Gospel of St. John informs us, and stayed with Him throughout the night. St. Andrew was one of them.[89] He was so pleased that he went to seek his brother Peter—then called Simon—and said: "We have found the Messiah."[90] This was followed by St. Peter's encounter with Jesus, when Jesus said to him: " 'You are Simon the son of John? You shall be called Cephas' (which means Peter)."[91] Our role as Christians is usually similar to that of St. Andrew: we encounter the Lord and then we go and bring other people to Jesus. Christians should not be turned inward. Our faith should make us go out of ourselves and become missionaries so as "to be witnesses of a Church open to the world."[92]

Another Gospel encounter is that of St. Philip, who after his first encounter with Jesus goes to recruit his friend Nathanael. Both of them, of course, became disciples. Then there is the encounter of the Samaritan woman.[93] At a certain point during the meeting,

[89] John 1:37–40.
[90] John 1:41.
[91] John 1:42.
[92] Massimiliano Menichetti, "Parolin: The Pope Asks Us to Be Witnesses of a Church Open to the World," Vatican News, September 10, 2021, https://www.vaticannews.va/en/vatican-city/news/2021-09/cardinal-parolin-interview-pope-francis-witness-journey.html.
[93] John 4:1–42.

she found herself in difficulty and tried to play the theologian: "Our fathers worshiped on this mountain; and you say that in Jerusalem is the place where men ought to worship." Jesus responded by asking her to fetch her husband. In other words, He confronted her with the truth of who she really was due to her checkered past. Having encountered Jesus, she went to proclaim Him to those in the city: "He told me all that I ever did." "Can this be the Christ?" Ironically, this public sinner is the first foreigner who became a missionary of Christ!

There is the encounter of one of the ten healed lepers—another foreigner, a Samaritan—who returned to Jesus to express his gratitude.[94] Another is the encounter of that woman who, sick for twelve years from bleeding, thought, "If I only touch his garment, I shall be made well," and she encountered Jesus.[95] And finally, there is the encounter of the possessed man from whom Jesus cast out many demons, which took over the nearby herd of swine.[96] After he was healed, the demoniac wanted to follow Jesus, but Jesus told him: "Return to your home, and declare how much God has done for you." In other words, tell everyone that you have been healed physically and forgiven spiritually. He made the man a missionary.

Many meetings reported in the Gospels show that the Lord looks for us and invites us to have a personal encounter with Him. Perhaps we lost the memory of when we first met Jesus and pledged our love for Him. So, we should ask ourselves: When did I first encounter Jesus, or when has Jesus encountered me? Surely, Jesus encountered us on the day of our Baptism, though most of us at the time were

---

[94] Luke 17:11–19.
[95] Matt. 9:20–22; Mark 5:25–24; Luke 8:43–48.
[96] Matt. 8:28–34; Luke 8:26–39.

little babies and understandably were not aware of this encounter. With Baptism, the Lord made us part of His people—the Church on earth, in Purgatory, and in Heaven.

As we grew older, all of us have had some encounter with Him in our life, a true encounter, when "I felt that Jesus was looking at me." This experience is not restricted to very holy people. If we do not remember it, it will be beautiful to think back and ask the Lord to remind us, because He remembers, He recalls our encounter. When speaking to the prophet Jeremiah, the Lord said to him: "I remember the devotion of your youth, your love as a bride."[97] It refers to that enthusiastic initial encounter, that new encounter.

Jesus never forgets, but many of us forget our encounter with Him. So, we should dedicate a few moments and ask ourselves: When did I truly feel the Lord near me? We should think of when we felt we needed to change our lives or to be better or to forgive a person, and when we heard the Lord asking us something. In other words, when we encountered the Lord. Our faith is, in fact, an encounter with Jesus, and this is precisely the foundation of faith: I encountered Jesus like Saul. Was it the time when the Risen Lord met me at Holy Mass, at Holy Communion, or when I was sick, or felt lost, or was grieving?

It might be that some of us cannot remember our encounter with the Lord, for it was so long ago—when we made our First Holy Communion, or when we went to Holy Mass as teenagers, or when we heard a homily that touched us to the core. Then it is important to ask for this grace: Lord, when did I consciously find You? When did You tell me something that changed my life or invited me to take that step forward in life? When we remember, we should rejoice in that recollection, for it was a celebration of love.

[97] Jer. 2:2.

The Lord always wants to encounter us, for He wants a personal relationship with us. Thus, Jesus comes down from Heaven in Person at the celebration of Holy Eucharist in order to change us from the inside. For He assures us: "He who eats my flesh and drinks my blood abides in me, and I in him."[98] He changes us to become more loving, more forgiving, more merciful, more authentic Christians. This is what really matters.

[98] John 6:52–59.

3

The Mercy of God

God's Mercy Gives Us the Strength to Cope with Life

The young Church, after the Holy Spirit descended upon the apostles on the first Pentecost,[99] experienced joy and apprehension. The joy came from the fact that the men and women gathered in the Upper Room, some 120, were afraid until the extraordinary event. Jesus of Nazareth had performed many miracles of healing, raised people from the dead, forgiven sins, and taught about love and forgiveness and mercy. He was initially very popular, but when He began explaining what is entailed in following Him and the meaning of His teachings, most of the followers fell by the wayside, because this was too much for them and it did not fit within their life's program.[100] In the end, the antagonistic Jewish religious and political leaders succeeded in having Him silenced by crucifixion. But Jesus rose from the dead, and then appeared to many, and ate with some of them to prove

---

[99] Acts 2:1–13.
[100] John 6:66.

that He was not a ghost.[101] Nevertheless, although now joyful, they remained afraid and relegated themselves to a secure place, the Upper Room. The scene of the Crucifixion was still very vivid and could not be erased, just as His appearance to them after the Resurrection could not take away the sufferings He had endured because the wounds in His hands and feet and the opening in His side remained in His glorified body. Perhaps they fixed their attention on the Crucified Jesus and saw in Him the price of sins. Perhaps they listened to His mother Mary, who encouraged and sustained them with her prayers. Now, thanks to the Spirit of Pentecost, the men in the group had become courageous and began preaching Jesus Christ as the true long-awaited Messiah and Lord, and many people came to believe in Jesus. There was every good reason to be joyful.

Their apprehension was rooted in the persecution that had broken out after the apostles began preaching. St. Peter and other apostles were imprisoned. St. Stephen the deacon was stoned to death. All of this was done by fellow Jews, such as Saul. They posed the question: If this is truly such good news, then why this opposition and persecution from the very people who know what the Sacred Scripture says about the Messiah? It did not make any sense!

Yet, what happened to Jesus' disciples is precisely what happened to Jesus Himself. Our Lord willingly ran to meet those sufferings foretold of Him in the Sacred Scriptures. He had clued His disciples in on those sufferings over and over. He had rebuked St. Peter for refusing to accept His Passion. He was crystal clear about the world being saved through His sufferings. Jesus did much good work, but in the end, He was executed as a criminal. People

---

[101] Luke 24:39.

had chosen Barabbas instead of Jesus.[102] The fallen children of Eve once again chose evil instead of good.

However, when the persecution of the nascent Church began, something marvelous happened as a result of rejection and suffering. Christ's disciples scattered. Some went to Antioch and preached in the synagogues to fellow Jews, while others went to preach in other places. The result of the persecution was that the disciples fulfilled the Lord's command: go and preach to all peoples, baptizing them in the name of the Father, and of the Son, and of the Holy Spirit.[103] In other words, the Church started becoming universal.

What did they preach? Jesus, the Son of God made man, had come to save humanity, and God extended His loving mercy to all. It is a mercy offered not only to Jews, but to the whole human race. The Church Father Tertullian (ca. 155-230) from the Roman province of North Africa wrote about the first Christian communities: "They were founded by the apostles themselves, who first preached to them by what is called the living voice and later by means of letters."[104] He had in mind both the oral tradition and the written New Testament.

We have much to learn from the first Christians. On paper, we in the United States have the constitutional rights of freedom of religion and freedom of worship. Truth be told, however, this is not the case, because there is still much prejudice against the Catholic Church. Also, we are divided as Catholics. Some pick and choose which Church teachings to follow, as if the tenets of our Faith are up for grabs or determined by polls. Some Catholics

---

[102] Luke 23:18-19, 25; John 18:40.

[103] Matt. 28:19.

[104] Tertullian, *Treatise on the Prescription of Heretics*, 20:1-9; 21:3; 22:8-10.

deal with others in a very unchristian way. We do not imitate God's mercy. We give up too easily when things do not go our way, when God does not answer our prayers according to our plans, when we refuse to give someone a second chance. We get discouraged and perhaps even disgusted.

How many times do we have to forgive the same person for repeating the same thing that hurts us or annoys us or angers us? Well, the Lord simply states that God forgives us without the limits of counted times. Forgiveness and mercy have no memory. In other words, each time we forgive from the heart, we give the chance to the other person as if this is the first time we are doing so. When we forgive, we imitate God.[105] We also imitate the Church, for, like a loving mother, she knows well our human limitations but never denies forgiveness to any of her repentant children.[106] This is affirmed by St. Athanasius, bishop of Alexandria (328–373), one of the great defenders of the Church against the heresy of Arianism: "Now through the grace of God's Word everyone is made abundantly clean."[107]

St. Claude de la Colombière (1641–1682) was the confessor and spiritual director of St. Margaret Mary Alacoque (1647–1690). Both lived when the Catholic Church was undergoing a spiritual renewal in France following the Council of Trent. When Margaret Mary told Claude that she had a vision of the Sacred Heart, he wanted to be sure it was a legitimate apparition. So, he told her, ask Jesus what sins you have confessed. The next time Jesus appeared to her, she did ask. She told Colombière. He did not know. Colombière said that the vision was genuine, for God has no

---

[105] Matt. 6:14.
[106] Heb. 1:3.
[107] St. Athanasius, *Epistle 14*.

memory of forgiven sins. In other words, God in His mercy forgives our sins and forgets them because He gives us a new beginning.

That is why we should never be depressed at confessing the same sins over many years. We are creatures of habit, and so we fall into sin frequently. God, in His mercy, picks us up and says, "This is a brand-new beginning." It is similar to our writing all of our sins on sand, and then the great tide of God's mercy rolls in and erases what we have written. Pope Francis, at the end of the Holy Year of Mercy, stated during his homily that God "is ready to completely and forever cancel our sin, because His memory—unlike our own—does not record evil that has been committed or keep score of injustices experienced. God has no memory of [any forgiven] sin, but only of us, of each of us, we who are his beloved children."[108]

Many a time we get upset at ourselves and at others because all of us seem to repeat the same failings. We turn to God as if He is our problem solver. We want to control God and tell Him how He should change other people—at home, at work, in our neighborhood, in our parish, and in society at large. If God would only change *that* person, *I* could become holier myself. Yet all of us, no matter who we are, change very slowly. It is similar to a housewife baking a cake. If she takes the cake out of the oven too soon, it is not done. If she leaves the cake in the oven too long, it is burned. We simply have to wait patiently for the correct time, for God's time to act.

This means we must be as patient and merciful toward others—and ourselves—as God is to us. To do so, we must pray for good coping skills. We must learn to cope with reality, with ourselves,

---

[108] Pope Francis, Homily at the end of the Jubilee of Mercy (November 20, 2016).

with others. Coping is a grace that helps us accept what is and live with it, praying and hoping and persevering until things get better, not according to our expectations but according to God's plan. The first Christian disciples went beyond discouragement and disappointment and frustration. They coped, and in coping, they became great missionaries.

Mercy Is Not Some Imaginary Thing

I had a great-aunt who lived in New York from 1924 until her death in 1980, one day shy of her hundredth birthday. My siblings and I, as well as our cousins, always got excited when she came to visit or when we went to visit her. She gave us sweets—and she smoked! We were fascinated with her and loved her deeply. Yet, she was very disciplined and predictable. We knew what she was doing at any given hour of the day. And there were three sacrosanct things that we were not allowed to interrupt: her preparation for morning 7:30 a.m. Holy Mass, even in snow, her recitation of the Rosary at 9:00 a.m., and her watching of her favorite soap operas on television.

In her mind, these soap operas just about reflected life itself. She knew who were the bad and the good guys. Everything was clear-cut, though she knew from her long lifetime that life and love were a little bit more complicated than her programs. But, I ask, why do millions of people watch these programs every day? Why do so many people identify themselves with some character in that daily thirty-minute show? I suspect that it is because we want to live life as if everything is in black and white. Yet this is a fantasy!

We must distinguish between true love and the love imagined for us on soap operas and in the movies. We can touch with our hands and see with our eyes the results of true love. They are concrete, for they are deeds and not simply words. The loving service to neighbor cannot wait until tomorrow. Jesus indicates this very clearly by not waiting until the beginning of the week to cure the lame man. Throughout the Gospels, he performs eighteen healing miracles on the Sabbath, fully aware that He will be greatly criticized and resented by His opponents.

The Lord invites us to live in His love, that is, in the love that God the Father has toward Him. He tells us that "as the Father has loved me; so have I loved you; abide in my love."[109] In other words, God teaches us about true love, which does not turn in to oneself, that is egocentric. The promise that God made to Israel that He would send a Messiah moved from words to action, from promise to reality. It was concrete. Thus, the Son of God became man and set His tent by dwelling among us.[110] God became one of us, and Jesus walks with us and has died for us.

The Gospels give us many examples of true love. St. John declares, "God so loved the world [us] that he gave his only Son."[111] Jesus told the young doctor of the law, a good man, but attached to his success and material possessions, to sell everything and then follow Him.[112] What Jesus did was to send this good man back to the world and its values, divest himself of all that is earthly, and follow Him in total freedom with an undivided heart.

Mark well that Jesus never imposes His will on us. There is always a choice that must have a concrete response. The young man must choose between his love for material things and his love for Jesus.

There is also the Parable of the Good Samaritan[113] that states that "to love one's neighbor as oneself" goes beyond recognizing

---

[109] John 15:9–11.
[110] John 1:14.
[111] John 3:16.
[112] Matt. 19:21–22; Luke 18:22.
[113] Luke 10:25–37.

someone in distress. It is not enough to feel pity for someone. We must respond in a concrete way, like the Samaritan, the man whom the Jews held as a great sinner and in utter contempt, yet who looked after the needs of the wounded Jew, took him to an inn, and paid his medical expenses.

After giving the parable, Jesus said to His audience, "Go and do likewise." In other words, do not simply pay lip service to the commandment "You shall love the Lord your God with all your heart, and with all your soul.... You shall love your neighbor as yourself."[114] We have to show our love for God by concrete acts toward helping the neighbor who is in need, whatever kind of need — spiritual, emotional, financial, and so forth. We have to help our neighbor become a better, holier person.

Likewise, true love changes us concretely for the better and makes us more holy. Many a time, true love involves suffering, forgiveness, mercy, silence, pain. It is as concrete as the love that compelled Jesus to carry His Cross for the sake of our salvation. In a way, Jesus, carrying the Cross on His way to Calvary, turns His head and gaze toward us and says, "True love is what I am doing for you!"

Jesus provides us with a program of how we can show our true love for God and neighbor in very concrete ways. He presents us with the Beatitudes: feed the hungry, clothe the naked, comfort the sick, visit prisoners, and so forth.[115] Thus, true love has flesh.

A friend from New York wrote to me and told me that we are surrounded with the poor. Some of them have very serious mental problems and cannot be helped by giving them money. Others, like the alcoholic or drug addict, would spend the money

---

[114] Matt. 22:37-40; Mark 12:30-31; Luke 10:27.
[115] Matt. 5:1-12; Luke 6:17-26.

by giving in to their dependency. He went on to write that there are many ways in which we can really help these people. One way is to acknowledge their presence—a smile or a kind word can go a long way. A small gesture of kindness affirms their basic human dignity and allows them to encounter the love of God.

This is what love is. It is communicated, not isolated. Imagine a married couple who claims to love one another, but does not communicate their love to each other. Imagine telling your children that you love them, but you never show that love. This happens all the time, and it is disastrous! True love is never isolated, never kept within us. We must communicate it through our deeds. A good parent will listen to their children, spend time with them, work to clothe and feed them, see to their education, tend them when they are sick, celebrate their successes, console them when they fail, and protect them from harm. We might think that the worst thing that parents can do to their children is to beat or berate them, to make them feel insecure and unloved—we all know these things are deplorable. But there is an equally grave thing that they can inflict, and that is when they do not show the children their love at all. They do not have to physically abuse them or fail to provide for them. The same thing applies when it comes to Jesus' love of us: He does not simply say, "I love you," but He shows it—never more powerfully than on the Cross.

Showing love is always taking a risk of being rejected. Just think of a time when someone you love was mad at you and you tried to show them you care. He or she might have rejected your love, your caring. This happens frequently in families, among spouses and siblings, between parents and children, among friends and coworkers. Reaching out in this way is risky because the other person might not accept our effort. Hence, we risk rejection and make ourselves vulnerable.

Nevertheless, we must never be intimidated or be paralyzed by fear. The phrase "Do not be afraid" appears more than one hundred times in the Old Testament. It appears many times in the New Testament, such as when Our Lord said to St. Paul: do not be afraid.[116] The archangel said to Our Lady: do not be afraid.[117] The angel of God said to the shepherds of Bethlehem: do not be afraid.[118]

Fear is a way of living, an attitude that really harms us. It weakens our resolve and paralyzes us psychologically. At times, it manifests itself psychosomatically, with hives, heart palpitations, tension headaches, ulcers, high blood pressure, and the like. Some people are so full of fear that they never make any difficult decisions, lest they make the wrong ones. In other words, fear makes us very selfish, insecure, and self-centered, because we reject taking a risk, opening ourselves up, giving of ourselves, and becoming vulnerable. Fear is not a Christian attitude, for it imprisons our souls and our very lives.

The opposite of fear is love, and true love is found not in the movies but in Christian living. It shows us how much God loves us and how merciful God is with us, for He is always willing to help us stand up after we fall into sin, to give us a new beginning, filled with hope and trust, for we are truly the beloved of our Creator.

Mercy Means Paying a Price!

The Gospel of St. John informs us that the Lord says, "I do not pray for these only, but also for those who believe in me through their word."[119] We have inherited this prayer of Jesus. We have been

---

[116] Acts 18:9.
[117] Luke 1:30.
[118] Luke 2:10.
[119] John 17:20-26.

entrusted with His teachings. We are now called to proclaim them in words and deeds—and more in deeds than in words. Ancient tradition informs us that St. Francis of Assisi told his followers, "Preach the gospel at all times; when necessary, use words." Jesus, our Lord and brother, is right now praying that we may succeed in this mission. The Holy Spirit helps us to do so.

All of us know that Jesus Christ is resurrected and has ascended into Heaven, body and soul.[120] Let us imagine Him standing before our Heavenly Father. What does God the Father see? He sees His only-begotten Son in front of Him, with wounds in His hands, feet, and side. St. Bernard of Clairvaux wrote, "He rose again on the third day, and showed the apostles the wounds of the nails, the signs of victory; and finally in their presence He ascended to the sanctuary of heaven."[121] In a way, Jesus is saying to the Father, "This is the price I have paid. Look at My wounds. Have mercy on them despite their many sins. They are Your children. They are My brothers and sisters, Your sons and daughters."

Jesus wants only good things for us, and yet He only asks one thing of the Father on our behalf: "that they may all be one; even as thou, Father, art in me, and I in thee, that they also may be in us"![122] Now that is interesting! What does being one with Jesus mean? Well, it rejects anything that has the spirit of the world, the spirit of the devil, the spirit of division (in fact, it might be recalled that the word *devil* comes from the Greek word meaning "the divider"). And how does the devil divide us? First of all, he tries to separate us from God's love and mercy. The evil one wants us to sin and separate ourselves from God and to give up on divine mercy and

---

[120] John 20:17; Rom. 8:34; Col. 3:1; Eph. 1:20.
[121] St. Bernard of Clairvaux, *De Aquaeductu.*
[122] John 17:21.

forgiveness so that we remain in despair, devoid of hope. But the devil does not stop with our relationship with God. He also wants us to be separated from one another in our proper family, in our parish, at work, in our neighborhood, in our country, and in the world at large. We just have to think, for example, of Christians fighting one another as a result of the unwarranted invasion of Ukraine by Russia. The evil one wants us to fall into despair so that we will not hear Jesus saying to us, "I know you have sinned, but I will pick you up again, I will forgive you, for I am merciful."

In fact, this division begins when we are still very small: I want your toys; then, I want your clothes; then, I want your room. Next, as we grow older: I want your looks, your smarts, your friends, your grades, your popularity, and I want to be the teacher's pet instead of you. Then, as young adults: I want your house, your car, your jewelry and money. Then, as we mature into adulthood: I want your job and economic success, your spouse or fiancée. Next, as we head toward our sunset: I want your health, I want your financial stability, and so forth. The spirit of the world makes us focus on what we want. I am so busy wanting what you have, how you look, who you are, that in the end I do not know who I am, and I am unable to appreciate what I have been blessed with. Such wants, focused on ourselves, divide and make us jealous, envious, hurtful, and scheming. They bring out the worst of us. They all go back to that first temptation in the Garden of Eden: the serpent asked them if they wanted to be like God.[123] Adam and Eve blew it, and we have to suffer from it because we are their descendants and the inheritors of their fallen nature. But other people also suffer when we want what others have. Adam and Eve forgot who they were, where they were, and what God had given them. They had

[123] Gen. 3.

suffered neither from cold nor heat, and were given dominion over all creation because God chose to entrust them with His wonderful creation. They overlooked that there were other sources for their nourishment. They just wanted what God had and who God was, and they sinned. I think we do the same.

Just as the devil brought a division between God and Adam and Eve, so the same devil brings division among us if we buy into his system, his worldview that is rooted and centered on selfishness. This is why it is all the more important to think of the prayer of Jesus for the Church, not in terms of some concrete building, but as the united family of believers, to which belong you and I, our family, friends, coworkers, and our parish. Jesus prays for people and not for buildings, for we are the living stones.[124] He prays that we may be selfless and not egotistical, concerned about the well-being of others and not self-centered, supporting others and not tearing down each other with gossip, fighting, backbiting, harsh words, and devious schemes. The goal of the Lord should be our goal if we are to be His true disciples and members of His family. It involves leaving no room for division among us, not letting the spirit of divisiveness, the father of sin, enter us. And if he does, then we seek the Lord's forgiveness and mercy and work toward unity. He is always ready to forgive us. Jesus Himself gives us the way to accomplish this objective when He says, "Abide in me."[125] As Pope Francis said some time ago, Jesus prays for us with His wounds as He stands before our Heavenly Father.[126]

Each of us is faced with three ways of living our lives, each of which is expressed in the Gospel of St. Mark.[127] These are expressed

---

[124] 1 Cor. 3:9; 1 Pet. 2:5.
[125] John 15:4.
[126] Pope Francis, Homily at Casa Santa Marta (June 3, 2014).
[127] Mark 11:11-25.

by the scenes of the fig tree that has yet to produce fruit; of the greedy businessmen in the Temple who are thrown out; and of the man with a faith that can uproot and move mountains.

The fig tree symbolizes infertility, that is, a barren life that is incapable of giving anything to others, which is absorbed in itself and does not want to have its so-called peace disturbed by someone else's problems. Jesus looked at the fig tree and saw it as being infertile because it seemed the tree made no effort to bear fruit. In other words, it did not work so that others may benefit from it. It refused to share with others. Are we such people? Are we unwilling to help others, because we live for ourselves and do not need anyone or anything, because we are satisfied with what we are and have? Let us remember that Jesus condemns spiritual barrenness and selfishness.

The second mentality is represented by the greedy businessmen in the Temple area. They are unscrupulous exploiters and solely interested in succeeding in life at any cost. They exploit God's holy place: they changed coins and sold sacrificial animals, making a profit off the devout. Do we truly know and respect the rights of others, such as our employers, our employees, or our coworkers? Do we want to make a quick buck, even by cheating at work (e.g., getting paid for work we did not do), promoting ourselves by making others look bad, manipulating others to get what we want, or undermining legitimate authority? We have to remember that it is not only the Temple of Jerusalem that Jesus declared as holy, but that our very bodies are marked as temples of the Holy Spirit. Hence, Jesus harshly accuses those who defile the temple of the lives of others. He says to them, "You have made this temple a den of thieves!" Again, I suggest that our choice is based on how we perceive the mercy of God.

Then, there is the third kind of mentality that I hope all of us have or, at least, are trying our best to acquire: living a life of faith. Faith is not something like rose-tinted glasses. Rather, faith is a kind of glasses that provide us with the right vision — granted that none of us have a 20/20 spiritual vision. Faith provides us with a way of looking at life that no one, no medicine or drug, can give us. Only God can give us this, and it is a gift. Jesus said to His disciples that having faith in God will make us so powerful that if we were to say to a mountain "Move," it would do so! Still, many of our prayers seem unanswered, many of our expectations turn into disappointments, and much of our good will to help others improve seems not to push us forward. The answer might lie in the fact that we usually want results according to certain worldly expectations: health, security, and the like. But the glasses of faith correct our way of looking at our lives and the lives of others, at our relationship with God and our neighbor. This kind of glasses gives us a correct approach toward life: it helps us see things from God's perspective. Every moment we live is another opportunity to draw closer to God, to love our neighbor better, to prepare ourselves for eternal life. Every moment — no matter what happens during that moment — belongs to God, for time is a gift from God.[128] Each moment is a moment of holiness because our time is God's time. So, every time we are hurt, we turn it into a moment of forgiveness and charity; every time people tell lies or gossip about us, we see only an opportunity to show mercy. Every time we are cheated, we turn it into an opportunity to pray for that person.

All of us are sinful and imperfect. But we also are a people of hope because we believe in the mercy of God, who always gives us a new start. We should recall what Jesus tells us in the Gospels: "So if you are offering your gift at the altar, and there remember that your

---

[128] 1 Cor. 10:31; Col. 3:17.

brother has something against you, leave your gift there before the altar and go; first be reconciled to your brother, and then come and offer your gift."[129] This is the only condition, so that your Father who is in heaven may also forgive you your trespasses,[130] for the Lord is kind and merciful.[131] It is the lifestyle of an authentic faith.

God's Mercy Does Not Pin Us Down

I suspect that we always run the risk of failing to properly understand and accept the mercy of God because we ourselves lack mercy. To cure this spiritual malaise, we must become obedient to God in all things, not least of all in the second great commandment: love of neighbor. This includes the ones who hurt or dislike us, or are unjust toward us, or damage our reputation, or steal from us, or do not respect us, or cheat on us, or lie about and to us, or are jealous of us, or feel they must always compete with us, or put us down frequently, or embarrass us, and so on. We should allow God's mercy to reach out to such people through us. Needless to say, this is very difficult because our hearts are often as hard as granite. Still, it is always possible with God's help.[132]

It is interesting to note that one of the great men of the Old Testament was obstinate and initially resisted God. I speak of the prophet Jonah. He was truly pig-headed! Remember how Jonah acted when God gave him the mission to go to preach to Nineveh and invite its inhabitants to repent before it was too late. Jonah had his own ideas, and no one—not even God!—could make him change his mind. So, what did he do? Instead of going to Nineveh

[129] Matt. 5:23-24.
[130] Matt. 6:14; 18:35.
[131] Ps. 103:8.
[132] Matt. 19:26; Mark 10:27.

to proclaim the importance of converting to God, he fled in the opposite direction, toward Spain. But God did not give up on either Jonah or the Ninevites. Jonah was thrown overboard in the middle of a menacing storm.[133] We know the rest of the story: he was saved from drowning by a fish, which swallowed him. Eventually, it spewed him out, and Jonah made his way to Nineveh. Jonah preached so well, so much was the grace of God with him, that the city converted, did penance, and changed its sinful way of life. We might say that there was a true miracle here, because Jonah abandoned his obstinacy and obeyed the will of God, doing as the Lord had commanded him. Jonah set out to convert the Ninevites, but was converted himself.

Jonah's original excuse for not going to Nineveh was very interesting. He used God's own words against God by telling Him that he had fled toward Tarshish because he knew that He was a gracious God, a merciful God who is slow to anger and abounding in steadfast love. This is called *presuming God's mercy*, and such presumption occurs not only with God, but with spouses and children, parents and friends. We do something wrong on the assumption that, if caught, we will be forgiven.

But there is more to the story of Jonah. Despite the miracle of conversion, he was not very pleased with the mercy of God. Yes, the great sinners in Nineveh converted, but Jonah turned to the Lord and said:

> I pray thee, LORD, is not this what I said when I was yet in my country? That is why I made haste to flee to Tarshish; for I knew that thou art a gracious God and merciful, slow to anger, and abounding in steadfast love, and repentest

---

[133] Jon. 1.

of evil. Therefore now, O LORD, take my life from me, I beseech thee, for it is better for me to die than to live."[134]

We can hear the sarcasm in Jonah's voice. What he's really saying is, "Okay, God. I did what You asked. I preached. They changed their lives. Then you forgave them. And yet you let their sins go unpunished!" It seems Jonah, though he converted from being pig-headed to obeying God, still lacked mercy. He wanted the Ninevites to be punished, even after God had forgiven them. How often we do the same!

Jesus experienced this rigid mentality with the Jewish legal minds in Jerusalem. We are all familiar with the scene from the Gospel of St. John: a woman was caught in the act of adultery and was brought over to Jesus to pass judgment.[135] These pompous and rigid Jews, these learned men, these obstinate men, wanted the law to be carried out. The woman must be stoned to death, they said. They could not understand why Jesus did not pronounce a death sentence on the culprit, just as they resented the fact that this famous Rabbi in Galilee also ate with the much-hated tax collectors and public sinners.

These men forgot even the words of the Psalm that they prayed on a regular basis: "With the LORD there is steadfast love, and with him is plenteous redemption."[136] They forgot, and people like them today forget, that where the Lord is, there is also mercy. We, too, forget that God demands more than worship. When His mercy is poured upon us, it is poured upon our sins, our deficiencies, our small-heartedness, our miseries, our obstinate hearts. And we must do the same for others.

[134] Jon. 4:2–3.
[135] John 8:1–11.
[136] Ps. 130:3.

We must beware of the devil, the one represented as the alluring serpent in Genesis chapter 2. He plays tricks on us so that we, too, might become deadly serpents. These are frightening words. However, we can become like serpents if we forget or resist the mercy of God, while continuing to present ourselves as pious Christians.

Have you ever looked at a cobra or some other kind of snake? Its skin is beautiful. Some people carry very beautiful and expensive handbags or wear shoes made out of snakeskin. But that is where its beauty stops. The snake's skin is gorgeous, but the snake's behavior is truly scary, and it can kill us with one bite. We may be charmed or mesmerized or fascinated with the beauty of the snake's skin, but if we stop at the external, at that which we can see, we are in for big trouble.

The same applies to our spiritual life. Satan can make us believe that we have a beautiful outside, a beautiful prayer life, a beautiful Christian way of living. We may be taken in by what we see. We might think that people might be impressed with our spiritual "success." Remember how St. Paul was really upset with the Church in Galatia, the people who were so generous with him? He told them that they were acting as if they were bewitched: "O foolish Galatians! Who has bewitched you?"[137] You who were called to freedom, who has bewitched you? They were very impressed with themselves, but when they disagreed, or when someone crossed them, they became deadly. Why? Because they lacked mercy.

We must always remember that we are called not only to worship God on Sunday, to say our prayers, and to be good to others, but that we, like God, must also be merciful because, as already stated, God is merciful with us. When His mercy is poured upon us, it is poured upon our sins, our miseries, our small-heartedness, our

---

[137] Gal. 3:1.

shortcomings, our obstinate hearts. The Lord assures His faithful: "A new heart I will give you, and a new spirit I will put within you; and I will take out of your flesh the heart of stone and give you a heart of flesh."[138] We do well to imitate God's boundless mercy.

Mercy Is Given to Those Who Ask for It

I remember doing an experiment once, and the results were disastrous. One day, I asked a judge to show mercy to a first offender. Not only was the offender repentant of what he did, but the police report also included many exaggerated accounts of his crime, which were concocted by both the officers and the victim. I showed up for the sentencing to see what the judge was going to do. The alleged victim herself was there, and she declared that the police report was exaggerated and went beyond her embellished complaint. These "embellishments" also led the offender to be charged with a felony instead of a misdemeanor.

But it was an election year. The judge and the district attorney were more anxious to get reelected than to administer justice with mercy and seek the truth. It was a game played out at the cost of a young man's life and the integrity of justice. I remember the judge that morning acting in a very unprofessional, flippant manner. She flirted with some officers of the court before the proceedings began and handed down sentences for one accused after another. I was stunned and wondered how corrupt and shameful our justice system has become.

These officers of the law, including the judge, knew they had power and flaunted it unabashedly. Many of the accused had been convinced by their unimpressive public defender to plead guilty and negotiate their sentence. In each case, the judge simply ignored

---

138 Ezek. 36:26.

reality and gave the maximum sentence to every accused person as he or she stood in front of her. The judge simply declared the decision without any explanation. I was shocked.

Of course, the accused were even more shocked! I saw fear in their eyes. Most of them were young people, generally in their late teens or early twenties. The judge, seemingly thoughtless and callous, did not hesitate to ruin their lives. She did not give a chance to first offenders. Afterwards, I kept an eye on that judge. After the election, her conduct made a lot of sense to me because she was elected by just over one hundred votes. She knew that her job was at great risk.

Did her concern about her future justify her behavior as a judge? I would say it did not and that the judge will be answerable to God one day for the grave harm she has inflicted on young people who needed a second chance and could not get it because they were too poor to get a decent criminal lawyer. The judge came closer to a seat on the circuit court, but she moved further away from Heaven.

Someone who has never spoken ill of another for his entire life would qualify for immediate canonization. But such a person—apart from Our Lord and Our Lady—simply does not exist. Rather, all of us suffer from the temptation of pointing our fingers at others. In my youth, it was a standard joke that when someone did something bad, he or she would say, "The devil made me do it." Today, this is substituted with blaming parents, spouses, work, the weather, a headache, the social system, Covid lockdowns, and so forth. We want to disown our failings and sins and to create a quick excuse. But this is not the kind of Christian life the Lord has called us to live. We have to be courageous and take the first step to recognize our weaknesses, our mistakes, our failures, our faults, and our sins. Christian life is focused on following Jesus, who forgives and is merciful. Otherwise, we are on the fast track to becoming hypocrites.

Most of the readings at daily Holy Mass during the sacred time of Lent point to a common theme, a way of behaving. Jesus spoke and then put into action two very important things: mercy and forgiveness. We are continually invited to replicate them. We are constantly challenged to rediscover and seek compassion, kindness, meekness, patience, forgiveness, and mercy. We have to be generous with forgiveness. We have to be generous with mercy. When we feel we cannot do it, we should just look at the Cross. He did this for me! And then recall what the Lord said: forgive and you will be forgiven, give and you shall receive.[139]

We should be like St. Paul. How many of us remember what St. Paul did when his name was still Saul? Well, the first thing that he did after he became a follower of Jesus was to acknowledge his sins. The apostle told St. Timothy[140] that he praised Jesus the Lord for having chosen him and gave thanks and praise for being appointed to His service, though Paul had formerly blasphemed, persecuted, and insulted Jesus by persecuting Christians. He wrote in the same letter: "I thank him who has given me strength for this, Christ Jesus our Lord, because he judged me faithful by appointing me to his service, though I formerly blasphemed and persecuted and insulted him; but I received mercy because I had acted ignorantly in unbelief, and the grace of our Lord overflowed for me with the faith and love that are in Christ Jesus."[141]

St. Paul was speaking of mercy. When St. Paul was still Saul, he was constantly on the move, angry at those Jews who were following

---

[139] Luke 6:37–38.
[140] 1 Tim. 1:1–2, 12–14.
[141] 1 Tim. 1:12–14.

Jesus of Nazareth. He certainly was not a man who had peace in his soul, nor did he make peace with others. Being pushed off his high horse, he woke up to reality and saw Jesus as Jesus really is. And, again, the first thing he did was to acknowledge his faults. Now he was following the counsel of Jesus.[142] He saw the speck in his brother's eye, but realized that he himself had a log in his own. St. Paul realized that he first had to take out the log from his own eye, and then, seeing clearly, he would take out the speck that was in his brother's eye. Similarly, the first step for us is to acknowledge our faults. This should lead us to experience what St. Paul experienced and stated: "The life I now live in the flesh I live by faith in the Son of God, who loved me and gave himself for me."[143]

How do we discover the log in our eyes? The best method, I think, is known as the *examination of conscience*. We have to be brutally honest and painfully specific in facing our sins, as St. Paul was. This is very important, because if we choose to ignore our faults, we become hypocrites—or worse, we abandon the truth altogether. Rather, let us strive to be full of compassion, kindness, lowliness, meekness, and patience.

Mercy: The Arsenal of God

Many live under the impression that practicing mercy makes us weak, and thus, should we show our weakness, we will never be respected or our authority will be questioned. But, in fact, mercy is not something weak. It is a great virtue. Mercy makes us strong. Revealing that we have struggles and at times fail does not render us weak persons, but persons who, like the rest of humanity, struggle

[142] Luke 6:39–42.
[143] Gal. 2:20.

and pray for God's help. Weakness, prayer, and forgiveness remind us that without God's help we cannot go forward in life. St. Paul was frustrated with some unknown weakness, but he admitted, "For the sake of Christ, then, I am content with weaknesses ... for when I am weak, then I am strong."[144] There is also the ancient anonymous prayer from the depth of one's heart: "Heavenly Father, in our weakness, we can do nothing without Your help." This is a beautiful prayer that goes right to the heart of the matter, for we express to God our awareness of weakness, our complete dependence on Him, and we ask for His unlimited help.

Recognizing our weaknesses and our sins, and confessing them, is truly indispensable if we are serious about being Christian. Let us look at the case of Judas Iscariot and St. Peter. Judas held back the tears of repentance. St. Peter shed them profusely. The first led to perdition, while the second led to forgiveness. St. Peter wept like a child after he betrayed Our Lord. It is so easy and yet so painful to imagine that look in St. Peter's eyes as he stood in the courtyard of the high priest, having denied Jesus three times. Yet, he found forgiveness in his Redeemer.[145]

In this regard, we are also like children who are learning to walk. Parents immediately recognize that the toddler needs help, and the toddler, without using words, looks at his or her parents and asks for their help through a gaze. In fact, the toddler relies on this help. Then, one day, the falling on the ground becomes a thing of the past. Similarly, we cannot advance in our Christian lives without the Lord's help for the simple reason that we are weak and stumble and fall. It should come as no surprise that a child of God who eventually is standing erect must be careful not

---

[144] 2 Cor. 12:10.
[145] Luke 22:61.

to fall by avoiding temptation, for he or she remains prone to sin and is also weak in faith. Therefore, we should pray frequently during our waking hours: Lord, increase my faith,[146] for I fall, I sin frequently. Remember the man who brought his possessed son to Jesus to heal him? Jesus told him that everything is possible to those who have faith. The father replied: I have faith, but make it grow, Lord, for I am weak.[147]

All of us have been enriched with the gift of faith. All of us want to advance in our Christian lives. But if we ignore or are not aware of our weaknesses and sinfulness, we will all end up overpowered because we end up relying on our own resources. We must make the prayer for more faith with peace in our hearts because we are forgiven and we have forgiven others.

Is it a sign of weakness that we cannot make it on our own? Is it a sign of weakness when we ask for help? No! It is a true sign of wisdom and great courage. One has to be strong in order to forgive. But this strength is a grace that we have to receive from the Lord. The Holy Eucharist itself teaches us this fact: the Lord makes Himself weak for us. He takes on the appearance of bread at the risk of being desecrated, discarded, or received sacrilegiously. Yet He doesn't cower. He presents Himself to us. He prays for us. He forgives us. Let us learn from Him the strength of trusting in God, the strength of prayer, and the power of forgiveness. We need to pray constantly for the grace to forgive. If we act according to the values of the world, which demands an eye for an eye and a tooth for a tooth, then everyone will become blind and toothless! The entire life of Jesus spells out the truth of this power: trusting persistently in His Heavenly Father, forgiving unceasingly, praying constantly.

[146] Luke 17:5.
[147] Mark 9:23-24.

But the world has a totally different message and understanding of weakness and strength. The strong dominate others, are more powerful than others, and use other people's weaknesses to control or compromise them. Thus, other human beings are no longer perceived as human beings. They become objects to acquire, subdue, manipulate, and overpower. This is neither peace nor love nor respect nor fraternity. It is unchristian to its very core.

We are called to enter God's time and world. To understand God's time, our hearts must be free of negative influences so that we are able to receive the gift of grace and not be overcome by the loud worldly noises that invade our time and attention, drain our energy, and render us anxious and restless. We must safeguard our hearts in order to be aware when God's presence passes through them. God's time is holy, and the time God gives us should also be holy. It goes beyond the time we spend within the boundaries of a church building at Holy Mass or saying the Rosary or engaged in any other kind of prayer. Every one of our living moments should be turned into God's time. St. Paul spoke of this when he reminded his fellow Christians in Corinth that whatever they did, it should be done for the glory of God.[148] When we separate God's time from our personal time, we are in effect moving into the time of the world and entertaining the possibility of sin. This division may be a cause for generating scandal. We might mistakenly equate piety with holiness. We act holy in church and are terrible outside church. Perhaps this is why many say, "Imagine, so and so goes to Holy Mass and Holy Communion every Sunday and then does this or that to others — mistreats family members, is constantly fighting at work, derides people, thinks himself better than the rest of us!"

[148] 1 Cor. 10:31; Col. 3:17.

If we are serious about being Christian, we cannot afford such schizophrenic behavior. We should enter God's time. We have to allow God to pass through our hearts and find a home there, where He is able to set up His dwelling. Pope Francis tells us that St. Augustine spoke on this:

> I am afraid when the Lord passes—but why are you afraid if the Lord is good?—I am afraid of not welcoming him, of not understanding that the Lord is passing, in this trial, in this word that I have heard and moved my heart, in this example of holiness, so many things, in this tragedy that pierced my soul. Thus, the Lord passes and gives us the gift of holiness. So, it is important to safeguard the heart in order to be attentive to this gift of God![149]

In today's world, every waking moment seems to be drowned out by all kinds of noise: trash being picked up early in the morning, cars and trucks and buses moving, construction, lawnmowers, alarms, doors banging shut, water running in the sink and shower, phones ringing, music playing, television switched on, and so forth. These are sounds easy to identify. Some are very pleasant, while others are obnoxious and annoying. But there are other kinds of sounds, those which try to hold hostage our attention and energies. They aim to capture our hearts, our minds, our souls. They are the sounds of gossip, envy, hatred, anger, anxiety, cursing, cussing, vindictiveness, pornography, and so forth. They are the sounds from Satan and his world and time.

There are still other sounds, very positive ones, that also aim to capture our hearts and minds and souls. They are the Word of God, the celebration of the sacraments, prayer, and the call to

[149] Pope Francis, Homily at Casa Santa Marta (March 22, 2020).

holiness. All of the aforementioned sounds are to be identified, specified, and evaluated because they occupy our waking hours.

In order to do so, and in order not to avoid or push away or ignore any sound that comes from the Lord, we first must identify the sounds that come from God and are of God. We have to listen attentively, discern with deep insight, and choose wisely, so that our hearts will not fall in love with an idol and enter into sin. Such listening is done through prayer and meditation—in other words, entering God's time. He constantly speaks to us of His love and mercy, but these can be drowned out by unholy sounds.

Being a good Catholic involves more than going to Holy Mass on the Lord's Day and not breaking the Ten Commandments. When we limit ourselves to these activities, we are more like an obedient Catholic rather than a good Catholic. An obedient Catholic is the one who simply does not commit sin and turns a spiritual journey into a matter of avoiding obstacles. A good Catholic goes beyond these confines and grows in spiritual life, walking courageously with the Lord as an intimate friend.

Remember the rich young man?[150] He followed all the Jewish laws. He was obedient to God's laws but not completely in love with God. He did not want to follow Jesus, so he went away very sad, for he wanted to hold on to his worldly baggage. He wanted to walk alone and not to be told that it takes more than obeying laws that make us inherit the Kingdom of Heaven. He failed to recognize his attachment to the fruits of the world.

The Christian never walks alone. A Christian walks in the company of the Lord, along with the community of believers, the community of faith that is called the Church. It is not enough not to hurt Jesus and the Church by not sinning—we must grow,

[150] Matt. 19:16-22; Mark 10:17-22; Luke 18:18-23.

mature, and move forward. Pope Francis, during a general audience, stated, "We are not isolated and we are not Christians on an individual basis, each one on his or her own, no, *our Christian identity is to belong!* We are Christians because we belong to the Church. It is like a last name: if the first name is *I am Christian,* the last name is *I belong to the Church.*"[151]

I wonder if that honest young man ever recognized his weakness and eventually became a faithful disciple, walking in the Lord's company and within the Christian community, and sought the Lord's mercy—the arsenal of a loving and redeeming God. I hope so.

---

[151] Pope Francis, General Audience (June 25, 2014).

4

Mary: God's Mother — and Ours

Our Lady Speaks

Mary is the Mother of Sacred Scripture, for Sacred Scripture is the Word of God. And yet we might be surprised to know that the voice of Our Lady is heard very briefly in the New Testament.

We hear her first words during the event known as the Annunciation.[152] All of us are familiar with the beautiful scene of the meeting between Heaven and earth in the Gospel of St. Luke. The archangel Gabriel, God's messenger representing the world of Heaven, meets the young maiden Mary, God's chosen one from all eternity, who represented the world of earth. This historic meeting continues to be presented in art down the centuries by such geniuses as the creators of various illuminated manuscripts during the Middle Ages and the Renaissance, in paintings such as those of El Greco, Murillo, Paolo de Matteis, and Leonardo da Vinci, in all kinds of icons in the Catholic and Orthodox churches, and so forth. Poets since ancient times have written about this

---

[152] Luke 1:26-38.

marvelous event, such as in the hymn that goes back to the time of the great St. Athanasius of Alexandria in the fourth century: "Today is the beginning of our salvation, and the revelation of the eternal mystery! The Son of God becomes the Son of the Virgin as Gabriel announces the coming of Grace."[153]

The scene of the Annunciation depicts God speaking through the archangel Gabriel and a very young Mary responding in person. St. Bernard captured that encounter with a reflection during one of his homilies that seems to go beyond the very short meeting and hints at Gabriel, joined by an anxious humanity, waiting for Mary's response:

> You have heard, O Virgin, that you will conceive and bear a son; you have heard that it will not be by man but by the Holy Spirit. The angel awaits an answer; it is time for him to return to God who sent him. We too are waiting, O Lady, for your word of compassion; the sentence of condemnation weighs heavily upon us. The price of our salvation is offered to you. We shall be set free at once if you consent.... Answer quickly, O Virgin. Reply in haste to the angel, or rather through the angel to the Lord. Answer with a word, receive the Word of God. Speak your own word, conceive the divine Word.... Though modest silence is pleasing, dutiful speech is now more necessary. Open your heart to faith, O blessed Virgin, your lips to praise, your womb to the Creator.[154]

And the young Virgin of Nazareth responded: "Let it be to me according to your word."[155] Though her response is formulated in so

---

[153] The ancient hymn (*troparion*) for the feast of the Annunciation.

[154] St. Bernard of Clairvaux, *Homily* 4, 8–9.

[155] Luke 1:38.

few words, it will utterly change the history of all humanity—your personal history and mine. The walk of God among us as one of us, except for sin, began at that moment.

(As an aside, it's worth mentioning that Catholics who deny that human life begins at conception are in fact denying the moment when God became man, as well as the Immaculate Conception of Mary—both dogmas belonging to the Deposit of Faith. Hence, what they advocate is heretical.)

Mary, this young teenage girl of Nazareth, saturated with her love, faith, and trust in God, uttered in effect what her Son will be saying and doing for His entire earthly life: "I have come to do Your will, Father."[156] Therefore, while Jesus stands as the one whom His mother will follow and imitate in doing God's will, Mary stands as a model for us to replicate what she did. Yet how many times do we seek to do God's will? How many times are we afraid of doing God's will because we find it heavy and burdensome? And what is God's will for us? Simply put, it is to put on Christ[157] and abide in Jesus.[158]

The next time we hear Our Lady speak is during the scene of the Visitation.[159] This event, too, has been depicted down the centuries by magnificent artists, such as Perugino, Albertinelli, El Greco, Raphael, Ghirlandaio, Raphael, and Rubens. First God, through Gabriel, visits Mary in her parents' home at the Annunciation. Now the incarnate God, through the Virgin Mary, visits His people, represented by St. Elizabeth and her unborn child, St. John the Baptist. After St. Elizabeth's greeting, and the silent recognition

---

[156] Matt. 26:39, 42; John 4:34; 5:30; 6:38.
[157] Rom. 13:14.
[158] Matt. 6:33; John 14:15; Rom. 8:9; Phil. 4:6-7; 1 John 2:24, 5:12; 1 Pet 2:1-15.
[159] Luke 1:39-56.

of the unseen incarnate Word (Jesus) by her unseen child (St. John the Baptist), the young Virgin Mother uttered a hymn of praise, the *Magnificat*,[160] the crown of the songs of praise to God in the Old Testament, praising not herself but God and His love for His wayward people—the mercy God shows as He fulfills His ancient promises to Israel. And, as we all know, God goes beyond visiting His people Israel. Once the Word of God entered human history at the Incarnation, He was here to stay until the end of the measuring of earthly time. He remains so in an eminent way through His full and Real Presence in the Holy Eucharist.

When it comes to us, do we recognize the unseen Lord in other people, as St. John the Baptist did? Do we recognize Our Lord's full Presence in the Eucharist, going beyond what our eyes see, our hands touch, our tongues taste? What can help us recognize the unseen Lord? Mary, full of faith, shows us the way. We have received at our Baptisms the Spirit who overshadowed Our Lady. He opens the eyes of our souls.

The Gospel of St. John has a beautifully poetic way of presenting the Lord being with us. Jesus said to the apostle Jude: "If a man loves me, he will keep my word, and my Father will love him, and we [that is, the Father and the Son] will come to him and make our home with him."[161] On the other hand, in the book of Revelation, this is depicted by saying, "Behold, I stand at the door and knock; if anyone hears my voice and opens the door, I will come in to him and eat with him, and he with me."[162] Jesus knocks at the door of our life, seeking entry, as we will one day seek entry into Heaven by humbly knocking at its door as poor beggars.

---

[160] Luke 1:46–55.
[161] John 14:23.
[162] Rev. 3:20.

The third time when Our Lady speaks in the New Testament is the scene when she and St. Joseph discover Jesus, age twelve, in the Temple of Jerusalem.[163] Many artists have also put to color this scene, such as Gustave Doré, Paolo Veronese, Heinrich Hofmann, William Holman Hunt, Josef Kastner, Jan Steen, Jacques Stella, and James Tissot. The scene has an inherent movement. The young Jesus, that is, God's presence, was in the home of Mary and St. Joseph—thereby, the humble home of Nazareth became the temple that contained the presence of God. Then the young family went, as was their custom, to the Temple of Jerusalem. Jesus, God's presence, stayed in the Temple for three days. The presence anticipated what Jesus will state much later: "Destroy this temple, and in three days I will raise it up."[164] He was totally misunderstood by those who heard His words. The three days also prefigured the days during which the body of the dead Jesus resided within the bowels of the tomb, from which He rose on the third day.[165] This scene of finding the twelve-year-old Jesus in the Temple anticipated the Lord's presence in the sanctuary of every church. Next, the presence of God returned to the home of Mary and St. Joseph, reminding us that it is not enough to enter God's presence in our church, but we must bring Jesus to our home. We must also do as the boy Jesus did: remain obedient. In the same way, we should take Jesus to our own personal version of the home of Nazareth and carry out our Christian lives by being obedient to God and following the example of Jesus toward Mary and St. Joseph. No biblical verses record what Mary and St. Joseph told Jesus during His growing years into adulthood, but we are given the effects:

163 Luke 2:41–52.
164 John 2:19; see Matt. 27:40; Mark 14:58.
165 Matt. 16:21, 20:19, 27:62–63; Mark 9:31, Luke 9:22, 24:46.

"Jesus increased in wisdom and in stature, and in favor with God and man."[166] We can grow spiritually when we entrust our life and home to the guidance of Our Lady.

With these three New Testament depictions of Jesus being with us, let us now envision our family, friends, and community. The Divine Visitor will make our home His home, just like we extend hospitality to our loved ones. The Divine Visitor will come to our home, and we extend our friendship and manifest our love and esteem by sharing a meal with Him. But this time, the meal is not ours. It is His, for it is the eucharistic banquet. Jesus points to this eucharistic banquet as being celebrated in Heaven for all eternity.[167]

The fourth and last time that Our Lady is depicted speaking in the Gospels is at the Wedding Feast at Cana in Galilee.[168] This beautiful scene is also depicted in art down the centuries. Famous painters like Gerard David, Juan de Flandes, Garofalo, Murillo, Tintoretto, and Paolo Veronese have used their God-given talents to concentrate our minds on this wedding scene and to reflect on its application to our personal life. Our focus is many a time on the silent miracle of Jesus turning water into wine. However, this was the end result of another scene, another encounter: Mary, a most gracious wedding guest, told her Son that the wine had run out. This conversation between Mother and Son indicates that Mary was most solicitous of other people's difficulties. It seems the couple got married on a limited budget; Our Lady brought to the attention of Jesus that the wine, a basic sign of celebration, had run out. The Lord's response was that His "hour" had not yet

---

166 Luke 2:52.
167 Matt. 22:2–14; Mark 14:25; Luke 14:14–24, 22:16–18, 29–30.
168 John 2:1–11.

come, but, as a loving and caring Son, He was not about to ignore His mother's request. So, Jesus gave in to her wishes.

The second conversation is between Our Lady and the servants, who represent all of us. She told them to follow her Son's instructions. She sent them to Jesus, her son—a command that extends to all mankind through Sacred Scripture. And when the servants followed Jesus' instructions, a miracle happened. The same will happen to us when we follow the Lord's instructions: miracles will happen in our lives. Just as the servants who did not expect the water to turn into wine, we will also experience the unexpected in our lives.

Pope Francis offers us an instruction based on what happened at the Wedding Feast at Cana:

> The words Mary addresses to the servants come to crown the wedding of Cana: "Do whatever He tells you." It is interesting that these are her last words recounted by the Gospels: they are the legacy that she hands down to us. Today too Our Lady says to us all: "Whatever He tells you—Jesus tells you, do it." It is the legacy that she has left us: it is beautiful!... And indeed at Cana the servants obey.... To serve the Lord means to listen and to put into practice His Word. It is the simple but essential recommendation of the Mother of Jesus and it is the program of life of the Christian.[169]

Our Lady is silent throughout the rest of the Gospels, even at the foot of the Cross. But when she spoke, great things happened that transformed the history of humanity as well as personal lives. From saying to the Father, "I will do God's will" at the Annunciation, she

---

[169] Pope Francis, General Audience (June 8, 2016).

ends with saying to humanity, "You must do the same." Her whole life, as depicted in the Gospels, is a tapestry of doing God's will. As the Mother beheld her Son on the way to His Cross, as she stood at the foot of the Cross on which her Son was being executed, her heart silently said: "Your will be done!" Her heart was still in God.

Ancient Councils and the Church Fathers Speak

Our Lady occupies a uniquely prominent place in the Church from her very inception as the household of God. St. Paul describes the Church as the Body of Christ.[170] Pope Emeritus Benedict XVI stated that we cannot separate the Church and the Body of Christ, for they are one. He taught that "in fact, only through Christ can we converse with God the Father as children, otherwise it is not possible.... It is in the Church that we discover Christ, that we know him as a living Person. She is 'his Body,' "[171] and that "Christ, the Fathers said, as the Head, is inseparable from his Body which is the Church, forming with her, so to speak, a single living subject."[172]

Following this line of reasoning, one can say the Mary is the Mother of the Church from the moment of the Incarnation, that the Virgin of Nazareth conceived the Church when she conceived Jesus, because Jesus and the Church cannot be separated. But Mary did not give birth to the Church. Rather, Jesus gave birth to Our Lady's sons and daughters, represented by the young St. John, from His pierced side,[173] symbolized by the flow of blood and water,[174] just like the birth of a child that takes place amidst

---

[170] 1 Cor. 12:27; see also Rom. 12:4–5;. 1 Cor. 12:12; Eph. 4:4.

[171] Pope Benedict XVI, General Audience (October 3, 2012).

[172] Pope Benedict XVI, Homily on the Solemnity of the Immaculate Conception (December 8, 2005).

[173] CCC, §766.

[174] John 19:34.

water and blood. These sons and daughters, in the company of Mary, were knit into the Church upon the descent of the Holy Spirit at the first Pentecost.[175]

The Teaching Church has declared four dogmas regarding Our Lady. They deal with Mary's personal relationship with God and her role in the history of salvation. The first dogma is that Mary is the *Mother of God*. It was declared at the Council of Ephesus in 431, in the midst of the then-raging heresies about the real nature of Jesus Christ. The second dogma is the *perpetual virginity* of Our Lady. This dogma was pronounced at the Lateran Council in 649. This, too, relates to Mary being the Mother of God and conceiving the second Person of the Holy Trinity without the intervention of a man. The third dogma is the *Immaculate Conception* of Mary. The dogma of the Immaculate Conception was declared by Pope Bl. Pius IX on December 8, 1854. The dogma essentially refers to the fact that God made the body of the young Virgin Mary as a sanctuary most holy and perfect, untouched even by Original Sin, in which the Son of God was conceived by the power of the Holy Spirit.

Finally, there is the dogma of Our Lady's *Assumption into Heaven*, body and soul. Pope Ven. Pius XII declared this Marian dogma on November 1, 1950, stating, "Mary, Immaculate Mother of God ever Virgin, after finishing the course of her life on earth, was taken up in body and soul to heavenly glory."[176] The dogma shows an indissoluble link between Mary and her Son on earth and in Heaven. These four dogmas form Our Lady's diadem. However, that diadem also contains other precious titles found in the Marian spiritual

---

[175] Acts 2:1–31.
[176] Pope Pius XII, Encyclical Letter on Defining the Dogma of the Assumption *Munificentissimus Deus* (November 1, 1950).

patrimony that bestow other factual as well as poetic attributes, such as are found in the Litany of Loreto, which was approved by Pope Sixtus V in 1587 and was last updated by Pope Francis on June 20, 2020.

When we read ancient Christian writers and look at some frescoes on a wall or ceiling of Christian catacombs, we see the presence of a deep devotion to Our Lady and the significance of the role of Mary in the history of salvation and in the life of the Church.

Distinct heresies in the ancient Church, even during persecution, revolved around the true identity and nature of Jesus Christ. In essence, some heretics claimed He was fully human, but became divine by adoption some time after His birth. Others went to the opposite extreme, claiming that Jesus is truly divine but was only human in appearance, and hence the second Person of the Blessed Trinity never became a human being, but appeared to be such. The Church's doctrine addressed not only the true identity and nature of Jesus Christ as truly God and truly man (the *hypostatic union*), but also the role of Mary. Was she the Mother of only the human Jesus or was she the Mother of Jesus as truly God and truly man? The authentic ancient Christian writers responded by addressing the divine motherhood of Our Lady, her perpetual virginity, and her relationship to God and to humanity.

St. Justin Martyr (110–165) is one of the earliest apologists who defended the Church's teachings against the false teachings of his time. He affirmed the dual natures of Jesus Christ: true God and true man, and the perpetual virginity of Our Lady. He is the first post-New Testament Christian writer to present Our Lady as the "New Eve" and Christ as the "New Adam."[177] Long

---

[177] St. Justin Martyr, *Dialogue with Trypho*, 100.

before the Council of Ephesus dogmatically defined Mary as *The-otokos* (Mother of God), St. Justin spoke of Our Lady's divine motherhood.

St. Irenaeus (130–202), bishop of Lyons and recently proclaimed Doctor of the Church,[178] spoke of Our Lady as the "Second Eve."[179] He called Our Lady an "advocate," an intercessor for humanity.

St. Athanasius of Alexandria (293–373) beseeched in one of his prayers to Our Lady: "It becomes you to be mindful of us, as you stand near Him Who granted you all graces, for you are the Mother of God and our Queen. Help us for the sake of the King, the Lord God Master Who was born of you. For this reason you are called 'full of Grace.'"

St. Epiphanius of Salamis (310–403) stated something remarkable about Our Lady being our Mother: "By giving birth to the Living One (Jesus Christ), Mary became the mother of all living."[180]

St. Ephrem of Edessa (306–373), who dedicated a number of homilies to Our Lady, had a very passionate prayer to Our Lady:

Blessed Virgin, immaculate and pure, you are the sinless Mother of your Son, the mighty Lord of the universe. You are holy and inviolate, the hope of the hopeless and sinful; we sing your praises. We praise you as full of every grace, for you bore the God-Man. We all venerate you; we invoke you and implore your aid.... Holy and immaculate Virgin ... be our intercessor and advocate at the hour of death and judgment ... you are holy in the sight of God, to Whom be honor and glory, majesty, and power forever.

---

[178] Pope Francis proclaimed St. Irenaeus a Doctor of the Church on January 21, 2022.

[179] St. Irenaeus, *Against Heresies*, 3, 19, 22.

[180] St. Epiphanius, *Panarion*, 3, 2.

Pope St. Gregory the Great (590–604) wrote about Our Lady being the Mother of God, echoing what was already dogmatically defined at the Council of Ephesus. She was also the handmaid of the Lord, who acquiesced to God's request that the Eternal Word take flesh in her virginal womb.[181] He recognized Mary's virginity before, during, and after the birth of Jesus.[182]

St. Ambrose (340–397) is considered as the Father of Mariology in the Western Church. Basing his teachings on Mary's being "full of grace," he went on to speak about Mary as the Mother of God, with Christ being the "flower of Mary"[183] ever Virgin,[184] who is the model of the Church in faith, charity, and perfect union with Christ. He wrote: "It was through a man and woman that flesh was cast from Paradise; it was through a virgin that flesh was linked to God.... Eve is called mother of the human race, but Mary is the Mother of salvation."[185]

St. Jerome (347–420), the genius biblical scholar, declared, "Death through Eve; life through Mary."[186]

St. John Chrysostom (349–407), like St. Augustine, was baptized in the Catholic Church as an adult. He suffered several exiles for his adherence to the Catholic Faith. He affirmed the virginal conception and birth of Jesus Christ, emphasizing both the Lord's divinity and humanity, as well as the perpetual virginity of Our Lady. In his Divine Liturgy, we pray: "It is truly right to bless you, O Theotokos, ever blessed and most pure, and the Mother of our

---

[181] St. Gregory the Great, *Epistle 11*, 67.
[182] St. Gregory the Great, *Homily on the Book of Ezekiel*, 2:8–9, *Moralia* 24,3.
[183] St. Ambrose, *On the Mysteries*, 111, 13.
[184] St. Ambrose, *Epistle 42*, 4.
[185] St. Ambrose, *Epistle 63*, 3.
[186] St. Jerome, *Epistle 22*, 21.

God. More honorable than the Cherubim, and beyond compare more glorious than the Seraphim, without defilement you gave birth to God the Word. True Theotokos we magnify you."[187]

St. Augustine (354–430), a convert and history's greatest theologian, was far-sighted in many things, including his teaching on Our Lady. He spoke of her as the Mother of God, as the Virgin Mother, as the Mother of the Church, and as the one selected by God from all eternity to be the Mother of the Eternal Word. He went on to plead in one of his prayers:

> Holy Mary, help the miserable, strengthen the discouraged, comfort the sorrowful, pray for your people, plead for the clergy, intercede for all women consecrated to God. May all who venerate you, feel now your help and protection.... Make it your continual care to pray for the people of God, for you were blessed by God and were made worthy to bear the Redeemer of the world, who lives and reigns forever.[188]

St. Peter Chrysologus (380–450) said, "Virgin, she conceived; Virgin, she gave birth; Virgin she remained."[189]

St. Theodotus of Ancyra (d. 446) emphasized the two distinct natures of Jesus Christ, fully divine and fully human, calling Our Lady the Mother of God, while remaining a virgin. By comparing Mary to the burning bush, which was not consumed, he taught that Mary's virginal body never underwent corruption.

St. Anselm of Canterbury (1033–1109) wrote three prayers to Our Lady. He implored in his third prayer: "Blessed assurance, safe refuge, the mother of God is our mother. The mother of

---

[187] From the Divine Liturgy of St. John Chrysostom.
[188] St. Augustine, *Sermones de Sanctis*, bk. 10, homily 18.
[189] St. Peter Chrysologus, *Homily 117*, 1.

Him in whom alone we have hope, whom alone we fear, is our mother. The mother of Him who alone saves and condemns is our mother."[190]

St. Bernard (1090–1153), a Cistercian abbot and Doctor of the Church, the last of the Latin Fathers of the Church, is traditionally ascribed to have penned the famous prayer the *Memorare*, which is still prayed today: "Remember, O most gracious Virgin Mary, that never was it known that anyone who fled to thy protection, implored thy help, or sought thy intercession was left unaided. Inspired with this confidence, I fly to thee, O Virgin of virgins, my Mother; to thee do I come; before thee I stand, sinful and sorrowful. O Mother of the Word Incarnate, despise not my petitions, but in thy mercy hear and answer me. Amen."

St. Bernard's special devotion to Our Lady prompted him to dedicate some of his writings to the Blessed Virgin Mary, such as the homily entitled *In Praise of the Virgin Mary*.[191] He addressed Our Lady as "Mother of Life" and "Mother of Salvation." He exhorts us: "In dangers, in anguish, in uncertainty, invoke Mary."[192] He went on to declare, "It is the will of God that we should have nothing which has not passed through the hands of Mary."[193] Likewise: "Such is the will of God, Who would have us obtain everything through the hands of Mary."[194]

The Church defines these dogmas, first and foremost, to give Our Lady the glory she is due. But we are also given these teachings for our own sake. The Church encourages us to turn to the sinless Virgin Mary and ask her to intercede for all of us sinners as our

---

[190] St. Anselm, *Letter to Gundolf*, 28.
[191] St. Bernard of Clairvaux, *Homily 4*.
[192] St. Bernard of Clairvaux, *Homily 2 on Missus Est*, 17.
[193] St. Bernard of Clairvaux, *Homily 3*, 10.
[194] St. Bernard, *Homily on the Nativity of Mary*, 7.

Mother. All of us who are baptized, though unworthy daughters and sons of Mary, are in need of constant spiritual conversion, whether we are great or small sinners. Great saints, recognizing themselves as being sinners, had recourse to Our Lady, the Refuge of Sinners.[195]

Our Lady's virginal example is also an antidote to the ills of our society. We in the modern West are plagued by grave disrespect for the sacredness of our human bodies. We are subjected to vast amounts of sinful sexual activity, the exploitation of women and children, and the rampant use of pornography. Many people think that virginity, sexual abstinence, and sexual control are fictions of the imagination and are irrelevant to our lifestyle. Let us turn to the ever-Virgin Mary to help us become pure in soul, heart, mind, and body.

We live in a culture that does not appreciate the noble vocation of motherhood, of the mother who empties herself to give her boundless love to her child. Our society, sadly, has developed an unhealthy perception of a child. Instead of seeing children as a gift from God and a source of great joy, the desirability of a child is judged in terms of expenses, professional aspirations, and personal freedom and comfort. Let us fervently pray to Our Lady, the Mother of God, to help us see the true meaning of new human life, the gift of a child, the blessing of a child, and of God entrusting new human life to parents.

As others have observed, we live in a "throwaway culture," where unborn children are discarded because it is mistakenly claimed that a woman has complete control over her body. God knows how many geniuses never see the light of day because they are aborted. Many unwanted pregnancies are mindlessly and violently terminated

---

[195] Litany of Loreto. The title goes back to St. Germanus of Constantinople (ca. 643–740) in the eighth century.

because a child might be perceived as a burden or a hindrance to the non-negotiable plans of a mother or parents, or as some unhealthy tissue that needs to be ejected from the mother's womb and destroyed. Even some Christians forget that Mary became the Mother of God at Jesus' conception. By Christmas, she had already been the *Theotokos* for nine months! So, let us turn to the Mother of God and plead with her to help stop the genocide of unborn human beings.

We also live in a society where death confronts us every moment, as the plague of Covid-19 and its brood continue to reign and rob their victims of life. We live in a society that seems unaware that we are created to live eternally and instead is living as if there is no tomorrow, no afterlife. Let us pray to Our Lady, assumed body and soul into Heaven, and beseech her to help us so that where she has gone, we hope to follow.

The Popes Speak

What do popes down the centuries teach about the Blessed Virgin and Immaculate Mary, the Mother of God and who reigns now in Heaven? Well, the response is found not only in the Marian dogmas[196] that form part of our Faith, but also in the many papal writings down the centuries. They indicate that Our Lady always lived in the stillness of God amidst a world full of turmoil.

I have presented in the previous section an outline of what the ancient ecumenical councils and some Church Fathers wrote about Our Lady up to St. Bernard. Now let's turn our attention to what some popes have written and said about Our Lady. The literature is vast, and it is not the present purpose to cover everything. Rather, I hope to highlight some aspects of Catholic

---

[196] These have been presented briefly in chap. 15.

Mariology, a discipline in the Catholic Church that deals with the doctrinal teachings of Church Councils, the life and veneration of Our Lady in the Church's life and prayer in ancient and illuminated manuscripts, in music, in art, and in architecture across the Christian centuries.

First, however, we must be sure that anything that has to do with Our Lady does not deflect or diminish our relationship with Our Lord. Recall that the phrase has been affirmed from ancient times: "To Jesus through Mary." That is my goal here, too.

Many popes down the centuries have greatly contributed to the development of the teaching on Our Lady and a deepening devotion to the Mother of God. The saintly Timothy Cardinal Manning of Los Angeles (1909–1989), while participating in the Second Vatican Council as one of the youngest bishops present, wrote:

> The Church is portrayed as God's family, founded on the Apostles, fed by His Body and His holy Word, reaching forgiveness, charity and holiness through humility and suffering. Seeing the Church through the image of a family, it is natural that God would provide a mother for it.... His Mother, radiant with all privileges and graces bestowed upon her by Him, is now held before the world as the mother of His family, the almoner of His mercy, the sanctuary of our sighs, our mother, our life, our sweetness and our hope.[197]

Our Lady is the Mother of God, the Mother of Jesus Christ, the Mother of the Church, our spiritual Mother, my Mother and yours.

The recitation of the Rosary is centuries old. Unfortunately, this beautiful devotion seems to have declined in popularity over the

[197] *The Tidings*, November 1, 1963.

last sixty years or so. Let us recall that Pope Leo XIII (1878–1903) was called the "Rosary Pope" for issuing eleven encyclicals on the Rosary! Furthermore, recent popes have consistently encouraged all of us not only to recite the Rosary, but also to recite it as a family, for the family is a little church, also called a domestic church.[198] Fr. Patrick Peyton coined and made famous the phrase, "The family that prays together, stays together," as he promoted the recitation of the Rosary. Perhaps we should ask ourselves: When was the last time that I prayed the Rosary, and when was the last time that I prayed it with my family?

Pope St. Pius V (1566–1572) was a Dominican and, thus, inherited the ancient Dominican devotion to Our Lady. He lived in a time when Christianity was in grave danger due to the expansionist program of the very aggressive Muslim Ottomans. As a spiritual son of St. Dominic, he wanted to further popularize the Rosary. He first did so by issuing his papal bull *Consueverunt Romani Pontifices* (On the Power of the Holy Rosary) in 1569, urging all Catholics to pray the Rosary as a defense against heresy. Next, as the dreadful confrontation between Christians and Muslims was coming to a head in 1571, he asked all Catholics in Europe to pray the Rosary. After the Ottomans suffered a major defeat at the Battle of Lepanto on October 7, 1571, a Christian victory that the saintly pope attributed to the protection of Our Lady, he established the feast of Our Lady of the Rosary, a feast we continue to celebrate today on October 7.

Pope Clement XI (1700–1721) was the Roman Pontiff who laid the foundation for the dogma of the Immaculate Conception of Mary, extending this feast—along with the feast of Our Lady of the Rosary—to be celebrated throughout the Catholic Church.

---

[198] Vatican Council II, *Lumen Gentium*, no. 11.

Pope Benedict XIII (1724–1730) added more indulgences to the Rosary and extended the feasts of Our Lady of Sorrows and Our Lady of Mount Carmel to the universal Church.

Pope Benedict XIV (1740–1758) was one of the brilliant popes. He authored a number of books on the Lord and on His Mother. He supported many Marian movements and increased indulgences for all who prayed the Rosary.

Pope Bl. Pius IX (1846–1878) was an outstanding promoter of Our Lady. He is the longest-reigning pope to date. His papacy was confronted with many religious, political, and social crises, including the suppression of the Papal States and the annexation of Rome to the newly established Kingdom of Italy. He was also the one who convened Vatican Council I, an assembly that had to be suspended—in fact abandoned—due to the outbreak of the Franco-Prussian War, the withdrawal of the protective French garrison in Rome in 1870, and the subsequent occupation of Rome by the troops of the newly established Kingdom of Italy. It was on December 8, 1854, that Pius IX proclaimed the dogma of the Immaculate Conception of Mary, binding all Catholics to henceforth assent to this infallible truth. The belief that Our Lady was untouched by sin, even Original Sin, had been taught since the earliest times of the Church before becoming an official Church teaching. This pope also granted the unanimous wish of the bishops from the United States to declare the Immaculate Mary as our nation's patroness in 1846, eight years before the dogma.

Pope St. Pius X (1903–1914) was the pope who promoted daily Communion and allowed children to receive the sacrament once they reached the age of reason and were properly prepared. He saw Our Lady in the context of restoring everything in Christ. He focused on the motherhood of Our Lady as being our spiritual mother and being the physical Mother of Jesus, the Son who has a spiritual and mystical body, the Church. Thus, Mary is also the spiritual mother of the members of the Mystical Body of Christ.

Pope Benedict XV (1914-1922), an underappreciated pope, promoted Marian devotion and wrote quite a few letters to pilgrims who went to Marian sanctuaries. He declared Mary the Queen of Peace in the midst of the devastating World War I. He promoted Marian devotions during the month of May, a month still dedicated to Our Lady. He outlawed, in 1916, statues and pictures that portrayed Our Lady dressed in priestly attire because the Church has never taught that Mary was a priest. Rather, Our Lady is the Mother of the High Priest. The Marian theology of this pope is so profound that he is quoted in the Dogmatic Constitution on the Church by the fathers of Vatican Council II.

The scholarly and courageous Pope Pius XI (1922-1939) marked the 1,500th anniversary of the Council of Ephesus by issuing a call to the separated Orthodox churches, inviting them to venerate Mary together with the Catholic Church and bring a close the Great Schism. (His call went unheeded.) He also established the feast of the Motherhood of Mary. He frequently quoted St. Bernard of Clairvaux: "We have everything through Mary."

Many people consider the venerable Pope Pius XII (1939-1958) the greatest Marian pope in Church history. He placed his pontificate under the protection of Our Lady in 1944, in the midst of World War II. He had been consecrated an archbishop by Pope Benedict XV on May 13, 1917, the date of the first apparition of Our Lady at Fatima. The connection between Pope Pius XII and Our Lady of Fatima never ceased. On October 31, 1942—in the midst of World War II—he privately consecrated Russia and the world to the Immaculate Heart of Mary. He made this consecration public and official in St. Peter's Basilica on the feast of the Immaculate Conception, December 8, 1942. Furthermore, he followed the same procedure that Pope Bl. Pius IX had implemented when consulting Catholic bishops, clergy, and laity across the world regarding the dogma of the Immaculate Conception of Our Lady.

Thus, after a vast consultation, Pope Pius XII, on November 1, 1950, defined the dogma of the Assumption of the Blessed Virgin Mary into Heaven, body and soul. He became the first pope to call a Marian Year, beginning on September 8, 1953, the feast that commemorates the birthday of Our Lady. He wrote about the special affection that the Blessed Mother has toward her children who are lowly, poor, afflicted, and marginalized. He encouraged and promoted Catholic educational centers to research and study Mariology.

Pope St. Paul VI (1963-1978) was elected during the Second Vatican Council. He was faced with a very formidable challenge in his contemporary Church. In his first encyclical, *Ecclesiam Suam*, he spoke about the devotion toward Our Lady, Mother of God, as being of paramount importance to live a life, for she is the ideal of Christian perfection.[199] Later that year, on November 21, 1964, he proclaimed Our Lady as the Mother of the Church during his speech at the end of the closing of the third session of the Council. He borrowed the title that St. Ambrose—who, like himself, once served as archbishop of Milan.

Paul taught in his brief encyclical, *Mense Maio*, of April 29, 1965, that the person who encounters Mary also encounters Jesus, for Our Lady leads her children to her Son.[200] He issued another short encyclical, *Christi Matri*, on September 15, 1966, presenting

---

[199] Pope Paul VI, Encyclical Letter on the Church *Ecclesiam Suam*, (August 6, 1964), no. 57.

[200] Pope Paul VI, Encyclical Letter on Prayers During May for the Preservation of Peace *Mense Maio* (April 29, 1965), no. 2.

Our Lady as the Mother of Peace, and confronted the then-ongoing Vietnam War and the dangers of atomic conflicts. He promoted the frequent recitation of the Rosary and on May 13, 1976, became the first pope to make a pilgrimage to Fátima.

All of us are very familiar with the unique devotion that Pope St. John Paul II (1978–2005) had toward Our Lady. His personal life and ministry as priest, bishop, and pope were lived under her protection. His coat of arms carried the letter M for Mary and the motto *Totus Tuus*: all yours. He attributed his survival of an assassination attempt on May 13, 1981, to Our Lady and travelled as a humble pilgrim to Fátima in thanksgiving, placing one of the bullets in the crown of the statue of Our Lady. He frequently wrote and spoke of Our Lady and fervently promoted the Rosary.

Pope Benedict XVI (2005–2013), during his address to the cardinals who had just elected him Bishop of Rome on April 19, 2005, entrusted himself and the Church to the hands of Our Lady.[201] He taught that the Lord and His Mother are inextricably bound together. Hence, Christology and Mariology cannot be separated from each other. He stated, when he was still the cardinal prefect of the Congregation for the Doctrine of the Faith, that "it is necessary to go back to Mary if we want to return to that truth about Jesus Christ, truth about the Church, truth about man."[202]

Benedict taught about Mary being completely at the disposal of God's initiatives in the history of salvation, as the supreme person who believed and hoped in the fulfillment of God's promise of salvation, as the woman who loves not only God but also all of

---

[201] Pope Benedict XVI, Address to the Members of the College of Cardinals, (April 22, 2005), no. 5.

[202] Joseph Cardinal Ratzinger with Vittorio Messori, *The Ratzinger Report* (San Francisco: Ignatius Press, 1985), p. 106.

us as she continues to intercede for us in Heaven as our mother. The pope's teaching on Mary is deeply rooted in Sacred Scripture.

Pope Francis (2013–) also has deep devotion to Our Lady. Time and again, he has shown himself to be completely confident in her intercessory powers. He always prays in front of the image of Our Lady under the title of *Salus Populi Romani* at St. Mary Major in Rome before departing and upon returning from every one of his papal pastoral journeys. In 2021, he dedicated the entire month of May 2021 to Our Lady's protection against the Covid pandemic, leading the entire Church in the recitation of the Rosary from a variety of Marian sanctuaries and churches dedicated to Our Lady across the world.

I participated every day in the Holy Father's prayer. What struck me most was that people from every culture, language, and ethnic identity throughout the world were praying to our common mother, Our Lady. That is why Pope Francis frequently exhorts the entire Church to pray to Our Lady, the humble Mary of Nazareth.

5

Which Sacrament Is for Me?

Baptism

The Lord, out of His abounding love, takes care of us from cradle to grave and beyond. He does so through grace, touching our innermost being, bringing the gift of stillness in our soul.

The seven sacraments, gathered around that of the Holy Eucharist, are sacred mysteries and means of grace. The Lord established each of them for our sake, not only to acquire holiness, but also to help us cope with the difficulties *this* life presents to us as we prepare ourselves for life eternal, when the curtain of our earthly time comes down and makes our bodies ready to return to the dust from which they were made.[203]

God's love assures us that no human being is ever alone from the moment of conception until death. No Christian is ever alone from the moment of Baptism until death. God is always with us.[204] He may be silent most of the time, but He is always present

---

[203] Gen. 3:19.
[204] John 14:18.

and guides us with His love, grace, and mercy. He is similar to an electric current that is always present, even when the switch is off.

So, which of the sacraments are for you?

The seven sacraments may be grouped into three categories. First are the Sacraments of Initiation: Baptism, Confirmation, and Holy Eucharist. They lay down the foundation for the life of every Christian. In the Latin Church, these three sacraments are received during different stages of life if we have not reached the age of reason at our Baptism. However, in the case of an adult, the candidate receives all three Sacraments of Initiation during the same celebration, usually administered during Holy Mass at the Easter Vigil.

The next group forms the Sacraments of Healing. These are the Sacrament of Penance and Reconciliation, and that of the Anointing of the Sick. All of us get sick, both spiritually and physically. *Sin* is just another word for this spiritual sickness. We need our sins forgiven, not only at Baptism, but also over and over again throughout our lives. We also need our spiritual and physical pain to find their real meaning and purpose.

Finally, the last group is that of the Sacraments of Commitment or Vocation. They are the Sacraments of Marriage and Holy Orders. They deal with the state of life of most adults.

We will discuss the sacraments in order of their reception. However, we will save the Eucharist for last—not because it is the least but because it is the *greatest* of the seven.

Baptism is the first sacrament to be received, and it initiates us into the adopted family of God, the household of God,[205] the Church. It is the fundamental sacrament, in that we must be baptized in order to receive any of the other six sacraments. Baptism is the sacrament of salvation. It allows us to grow and mature both in

---

[205] Eph. 2:19.

our spirituality and in our relationships. Therefore, this sacrament deals with our entire person. Just as we are born from our mother at the moment of our physical birth and enter the reality of the physical world, in Baptism we are born anew[206] on the spiritual level through our Mother, the Church, and we enter the reality of the spiritual world, established in an eternal unbreakable bond with God our Father.

Once baptized, we are spiritually marked not only for our earthly life, but for all eternity. No sin, even renouncing Jesus Christ (apostasy), can erase this mark from our soul. This is why the Sacrament of Baptism can never be repeated once validly administered. All of us know our physical birthday, and similarly we should know our spiritual birthday, the day of our Baptism.

Jesus Christ instituted the Sacrament of Baptism when He, at the time of His Ascension, commissioned the apostles to go to all nations and make disciples of their members by baptizing them "in the name of the Father and of the Son and of the Holy Spirit."[207] They were to be baptized by water and the Holy Spirit.[208]

There exists an unbreakable bond between Baptism and faith. In fact, at the very beginning of the rite of Baptism, the candidate, or those presenting an infant for Baptism, is asked what is being sought from God's Church. The response is "Faith." Baptism gives the person the seed of faith, which should grow henceforth in the fertile soil of his or her personal life. Faith needs a community or a family of believers wherein it is professed and develops, for the journey of faith is never traveled alone. We journey as members the Church. The parents of a baptized infant pledge to raise their

---

[206] 1 Pet. 1:23.
[207] Matt. 28:19.
[208] Acts 11:16–18.

child in the Faith. The godparents publicly and solemnly promise that they are able and ready to help the newly baptized, their godchild, grow in the Faith. The believing community, all of us who are baptized, is also responsible for assisting the baptized to develop that faith by inspiring the individual with our Christian lifestyle.

The ordinary ministers of this sacrament are bishops, priests, and deacons. However, Baptism is so essential that, in urgent situations, it can be administered by anyone, including a non-baptized person who has the intention of baptizing the person in the Church and using water and the Trinitarian baptismal words. The actual Baptism is administered by pouring water, and only water with no additives, over the head of a person, or by immersing the person three times in water, while the words "I baptize you in the name of the Father and of the Son and of the Holy Spirit" are pronounced. The Catholic Church teaches that the Holy Spirit enters the human soul at our Baptism, purifying it of all sin, including all sin committed by one who has already reached the age of reason at Baptism, and making the baptized an adopted child of God and member of the divine household. Baptism makes us participators in the mission of the Church, thereby becoming missionaries. By Baptism, we become a temple of the Holy Spirit dwelling within us.[209] Baptism renders us sharers in the universal priesthood of Christ, as well as in His prophetic and royal mission. This sacrament bestows a share in the common priesthood of all believers.[210] The presence of the Holy Spirit within the newly baptized bestows sanctifying grace,

---

[209] 1 Cor. 3:16.

[210] There are two kinds of priesthood in the Church: the common priesthood of all the baptized and the ministerial priesthood. The latter is the Sacrament of Holy Orders and cannot be validly received unless a male, and only a male, already shares in the common priesthood by virtue of being already baptized.

thus enabling us to not only believe in, hope in, and love God, but also to share in the supernatural life of the Church by growing in virtue and goodness.

Baptism by water and the Spirit is rooted in the Old Testament. This reality is brought out when the water for Baptism is being blessed, recalling the great events in the history of salvation by speaking of water as the source of life and fruitfulness from the very beginning of Creation;[211] new life that followed the Great Flood;[212] the liberation of the Hebrew people from their Egyptian slavery when God led them through the waters of the Red Sea;[213] and the crossing of the waters of the River Jordan that marked God endowing the Promised Land to Abraham's descendants.[214] The last event stands above all others. It anticipated the liberation that the Sacrament of Baptism bestows on its recipient.

The beginning of the public ministry of the Lord at age thirty is marked with His willingness to go to the River Jordan to be baptized by John the Baptist.[215] He did so not out of need. In fact, instead of the waters sanctifying the Lord, it was the Lord who sanctified the waters. As already stated, before the Lord returned to the Father, He charged His followers to go into the world and baptize people from every nation. The Spirit who hovered over the waters of the first Creation is the same Spirit who descended upon the Lord to mark the beginning of a new creation, as the Father revealed Jesus as His "beloved Son."[216] It is the same Spirit who descends into our souls at Baptism. Baptism gives us the identity

[211] Gen. 1:10–12.
[212] Gen. 9:1–3.
[213] Exod. 14:13–25.
[214] Josh. 3:14–17.
[215] Matt. 3:13–17; Mark 1:9–11; Luke 3:21–22.
[216] Matt. 3:17; Mark 1:11; Luke 3:22.

and name of *Christian*, and we become siblings to all living and past baptized Christians, not restricted to those who form the Catholic Church.

At Baptism, we arise as if resurrected with the Lord and emerge as new creatures on the spiritual level. This is done by the presence and power of the Spirit. The acquired purity of our souls is symbolized by clothing the baptized in a white garment. The newly baptized is also given a candle, which is lit from the Easter Candle. It signifies that Christ has enlightened the newly baptized, and in Him every baptized person is the light of the world.[217] The lit candle also symbolizes that the newly baptized will walk in faith through life in the light of Christ and until the Paschal Candle, lit at the funeral, is blown out, for there will be no longer the need for the light of the sun by day or the moon by night, because the Lord will be our everlasting light as we see Him face to face.[218] This relationship will never be exhausted by eternal time.

Of course, Baptism does not take away the humanness of one who is baptized. Thus, we remain susceptible to illness, suffering, weaknesses, concupiscence, and ultimately physical death.

The Holy Spirit who descended upon the Lord's followers on the day of Pentecost[219] has not left the Church since that day. It's worth noting that the Spirit descended upon them, not only as a group, but also as distinct individuals. This marks a new stage in God's plan of salvation. Unlike the case in the Old Covenant when only Jews belonged to the People of God, the New Covenant established by the Lord offers membership to all people. Henceforth, membership in the People of God was not restricted to physical birth into a

---

[217] Matt. 5:14; John 12:36; Phil. 2:15.
[218] Isa. 60:19–20; Rev. 21:23.
[219] Acts 2:1–4.

specific people. It would be conveyed, rather, by a spiritual rebirth. The reception of Baptism was thereafter connected with the gift of faith in the Lord.

St. Paul explained that through Baptism one enters into communion with the Lord's death, is buried with Him, is raised with Him to walk in the newness of life,[220] and now walks in the light of faith.[221] Bishop Faustus of Riez, who lived in the first half of the fifth century and was an avid opponent to the heresy of Arianism, wrote the following while commenting on the miracle at the Wedding of Cana in Galilee. He is referring to the water turned into wine, but also alluding to the changes brought about by the waters of Baptism:

> To those who see everything only with the physical eye, all the events at Cana are strange and wonderful; to those who understand by faith, they are also signs. For, if we look closely, the very water tells us of our rebirth in baptism. One thing is turned into another from within, and in a concealed way a lesser creature is changed into a greater. All this points to the hidden reality of our second birth. At Cana water was suddenly changed; later it will cause a change in man.[222]

Of course, one is not given the opportunity to accept the Lord's invitation if one has never heard it. Hence, Baptism is necessary for those who hear the gospel proclamation and are given the possibility to seek Baptism. But it's important to bear in mind that God is not bound by His sacraments. This is why the gift of

---

[220] Rom. 6:3-4.
[221] Eph. 5:7-8.
[222] Faustus of Riez, *Homily 5 on the Epiphany*, no. 2.

Heaven is not exclusively limited to the baptized. The basis for this is that Jesus Christ died for everyone, not only for the baptized. God's mysterious saving ways are never restricted nor conditioned.

A newly baptized person assumes new obligations and enjoys new rights. Firstly, we no longer belong to ourselves, but to Christ.[223] As such, we are called to serve others as members of the Church and are subject to those appointed as spiritual leaders of the Church. But we are also now able to receive the other sacraments, especially Holy Eucharist, to be nourished by the Word of God, and to be supported by the Church in varied ways so as to grow in holiness.

Confirmation

Jesus Christ instituted the Sacrament of Confirmation before His Ascension when He breathed upon His apostles and said, "Receive the Holy Spirit."[224] The third Person of the Trinity strengthens us by this sacrament in the *initial gifts of the Spirit*. We are enabled, as baptized Christians, to become authentic witnesses of the Lord and more responsible to spread and defend the Faith by word and deed within our contemporary historical setting and culture. The Holy Spirit equips us to carry out the mission by bestowing His sevenfold gifts: wisdom, understanding, counsel, fortitude, knowledge, piety, and fear of the Lord.[225] The Catholic Church teaches that at Baptism one receives the initial gift of the Holy Spirit and that it is at the Sacrament of Confirmation that the baptized receives His seven gifts.

The Holy Spirit descended upon Jesus at His Baptism. The same Spirit, in fulfillment of the Lord's promise, was first bestowed

[223] 1 Cor. 3:23.
[224] John 20:22; see also Acts 8:17; 10:44–48; 19:6.
[225] CCC, §1831.

upon His disciples on Easter Sunday[226] and subsequently on Pentecost to the faithful then gathered around Our Lady in the Upper Room. The dreams of ancient faithful Jews and the vigilant Jewish faithful at the time of the Lord had been hurriedly buried in a newly hewn grave. His few followers huddled together in the Upper Room, where fear and anxiety ruled. Yet, there was one candle still lit with faith and trust in Mary's Son, the Crucified One.

Beginning with the event following St. Peter's first homily at Pentecost to a multitude of people,[227] the Holy Spirit descended upon those who were baptized.[228] This nascent Christian community is succeeded by countless others down to our own time. The same Holy Spirit continues to descend upon us and will do so until the end of time.

Very early in the Church, the anointing with the oil of sacred chrism, consecrated by the bishop at the Chrism Mass, was added to the laying on of hands during the Confirmation ceremony, signifying that the baptized is anointed just as Christ had been anointed by the Holy Spirit.[229] The rite of anointing the Confirmation candidate with sacred chrism has been used uninterruptedly ever since.

The ordinary minister of the Sacrament is a bishop, but priests may be given permission to perform confirmations. The Sacrament is received by the laying on of the minister's hands on the head of the candidate, followed by the anointing of the forehead in the Sign of the Cross with the chrism while the words, "(Confirmation name), be sealed with the gift of the Holy Spirit" are pronounced by the minister. This sacrament may never be repeated.

---

[226] John 20:22.
[227] Acts 2:1–14.
[228] Acts 2:38.
[229] Acts 10:38.

It is customary in the United States to receive this sacrament during adolescence. However, the notion that Confirmation is a sacrament of maturity is misleading. At the time of administering the Sacrament, and indeed throughout our entire life, we are not fully mature in the Faith, nor does the anointing with the sacred chrism automatically produce such maturity. Rather, conversion to Christ, completely identifying ourselves with Christ, is a lifelong process. We are strengthened during this journey by the gifts of the Holy Spirit.

That is what Confirmation does. It strengthens us.

Since Confirmation is one of the Sacraments of Initiation, it is not only associated with Baptism but also with the Holy Eucharist. For many centuries, Confirmation preceded Holy Communion. However, in 1910, Pope St. Pius X made it possible for children who have reached the age of reason, usually around age seven, to make their First Holy Communion. This reversed the order of the reception of the Sacraments of Initiation in the Latin Church. Until 1910, Confirmation was seen as the sacrament that led to Holy Eucharist.

The anointing with sacred chrism signifies that those being confirmed are being imprinted with an irremovable seal of the Holy Spirit and consecrated to God. One meaning of a seal is that of being a symbol of belonging to someone in authority. The seal at Confirmation marks us as belonging totally to Christ.

The effects of Confirmation are an increase in and deepening of the grace of Baptism, a deeper grounding in being God's child, a firmer unity with the Lord, an increase in the gifts of the Holy Spirit, and a more perfect bond with the Church. Also, because all Christians are missionaries, the Holy Spirit further strengthens *confirmandi* to profess and be witnesses to the Lord in word and in deed.

The Holy Eucharist

The Lord Jesus Christ instituted the Sacrament of the Holy Eucharist during the Last Supper, the day before He was executed.[230] By instituting the Holy Eucharist, the Lord ensured that He personally remains present in the Church until the end of time. If this is not true, then I and all the Catholic priests and bishops in these two thousand years have wasted our lives and ministered as counterfeit clergy. All of us have been fooled by the Spirit of Truth—something impossible. As St. Paul would say, our faith has been in vain.

The Catholic Church teaches that the words pronounced by Jesus on the bread and wine during His Last Supper[231] are the *Words of Institution.* Through the power of the Holy Spirit, they transform the bread and wine into the Body and Blood of Jesus Christ without losing their outward appearances or physical taste. The essential signs of Holy Eucharist are wheat bread, grape wine, and the Words of Consecration pronounced by Jesus Christ during the Last Supper and repeated now by a validly ordained priest.

First, the bread and wine—what's known as the *matter* of the Eucharist.

If we go across the vast wheat farms of the United States, we will discover the source of the bread we eat. It looks radically different than the bread put in front of us. Bread, of course, does not grow in fields. It is only through a very complicated process that wheat is transformed into bread. The bread that is common to our sight requires a lot of hard work unseen by us. It serves as nourishment. The Lord Jesus took that transformed wheat and used it as a means to remain present in our midst. So, at the Last Supper, Jesus took bread, blessed it, broke it, and gave it to His

230 Matt. 26:17–29; Mark 14:12–25; Luke 22:7–20; 1 Cor. 11:23–26.
231 Matt. 26:26–28; Mark 14:22–26; Luke 22:19–20; 1 Cor. 11:23–25.

disciples while telling them: "This is my body."[232] He gave us food to nourish us on our journey to Heaven.

Likewise, there are some states that produce delicious wine. The most famous is that from California. Should we go to a wine region, we would behold endless acres covered with vineyards and, at the right time of the year, their branches produce lots of grapes. These look radically different from the wine we drink. As in the case of wheat, the transformation from grape into wine is a very long and complicated process. The Lord chose wine as a means of providing us with drink. So, Jesus took the cup of wine, blessed it, and gave it to His disciples, declaring: "This is my blood of the [new] covenant."[233]

Jesus is not only personally present in our midst, but He also supplies us with food and drink during our terrestrial journey. He remains our spiritual nourishment.

The Holy Eucharist completes the Sacraments of Initiation. It is the heart and the summit of the life of the Church. It is central to the unity and life of the Church. It is called the "Sacrament of sacraments," for the other six sacraments are oriented to this sacrament, for in it the Lord associates all the members of His Church to the one sacrifice of the Cross from whence the graces of salvation are poured upon all the members of His Church on earth.[234]

So many of the current controversies in our Church revolve around one question: Who should receive Holy Communion? Of course, no one is ever worthy to receive the eucharistic Lord. This is His gratuitous gift to us: the gift of Himself. Yet the Church has

---

[232] Matt. 26:26; Mark 14:22; Luke 22:19; 1 Cor. 11:23-24.
[233] Matt. 26:28; Mark 14:24; Luke 22:20; 1 Cor. 11:25.
[234] CCC, §§1324-1327.

made clear, going back to the age of the apostles, that one must be *rightly disposed* to receive the Eucharist. Otherwise, it can cause grave spiritual harm.[235] Still, all too often, laymen—and some bishops—place a desire for "inclusivity" ahead of good spiritual health.

The Church teaches that, in order to receive Holy Communion, one must (A) profess the Catholic Faith, and (B) live in conformity with Catholic teaching. Yet there is a movement afoot among "progressive Catholics" to admit individuals who do not meet these criteria. They wish to admit Protestants, homosexuals, and divorced-and-"remarried" Catholics to the altar rail. They also insist that pro-choice Catholics—including powerful lawmakers—be allowed to receive the Sacrament of the Altar.

If we *are* rightly disposed to receive Our eucharistic Lord, He comes down as the living bread from Heaven, and whoever eats His flesh and drinks His blood will have eternal life. He abides in us, and we abide in Him.[236]

The Holy Eucharist refers to two objective realities in the life of the Church. The first pertains to the celebration of Holy Mass. Only validly ordained priests are empowered to celebrate Holy Mass. The second reality is that once the bread and wine are consecrated, they become and remain Jesus Christ as His Body, Blood, soul, and divinity. The Catholic Church refers to this mystery as the *Real Presence*. The Church also teaches that the words of consecration of the bread and wine transform them into Jesus Christ Himself, though without changing the outward appearances and taste of the bread and wine. This is known as *transubstantiation* because the substance that makes bread and wine, their inner

[235] 1 Cor. 11:29.
[236] John 6:51, 54, 56.

reality, are changed into Jesus Christ, when He becomes present in His Body, Blood, soul, and divinity.

In encountering the Lord, fully present, the Holy Eucharist transforms us into better people, better Christians, better citizens. This means that we are not only spiritually enriched, but also changed for the better in our personal lives.

The Church encourages Catholics in the state of grace to receive Holy Communion during Holy Mass. We are commanded to do so at least once a year, but encouraged to do so every day. The Eucharist is given to the recipient as spiritual nourishment both in and outside Holy Mass. It is called Holy Communion because it unites the receiver with Christ and other believers. Any additional consecrated bread is put aside for silent adoration any time after Mass and also to bring Holy Communion to those who are unable to be present for the celebration of Holy Mass for a justifiable reason. The Church happily accommodates these people because a life devoid of the Eucharist is like a car that has no fuel. It can't get anywhere.

As I've already stated elsewhere, there seems to be something that does not fit when it comes to the celebration of Holy Mass. We are invited to ask ourselves: Why is it that for some people Holy Mass feels more true and more holy when someone very important celebrates it, as if it is not the same Lord who comes down from Heaven? What matters is that we are in the presence of Christ. If we do not focus on the eucharistic Jesus, we are becoming Christian merely in name, for our hearts lie elsewhere. We must fall in love with Jesus.

The Lord is present to us in many ways. He is present in Sacred Scripture. He is present in the ministerial priesthood when the priest administers the sacraments in the Person of Christ. He is present in the Church. Thus, He is present in our daily prayers, for

He assures us that "where two or three are gathered in my name, there am I in the midst of them."[237] He is present when He speaks to us through others, be they the Church ministers or some other persons. But these are glimpses of the *Real Presence* of Jesus Christ in the Eucharist, where He gives *all* of Himself—Body, Blood, soul, and divinity. He is uniquely present to us, to our local community of faith, to the entire Church, and to the whole world. It is the complete gift of Himself.[238] The same Christ is present in the monastic Low Mass, in a grand Pontifical High Mass celebrated by a pope or bishop or priest accompanied with angelic music and majestic hymns, in the diverse languages and cultures in which Mass is celebrated, in the prison cell of a priest in China or North Korea, or at the bedside of the sick and the dying. These are literal *re-creations* of what took place at the Last Supper.

Moreover, Christ is not a passerby just stopping in to visit His people. Our Lord remains present after the eucharistic celebration. He is Lord of time, space, and matter; therefore, He is not bound to these things in any way, shape, or form. There are not many different Jesuses present in the different Eucharists across the world, but only the one and same Jesus, fully present in each and every one of them. Similarly, there is no division of the eucharistic Lord when consecrated Hosts are broken up. Since the celebrating priest acts in the Person of Christ (*in Persona Christi*), the eucharistic Christ is not only the minister of this Sacred Sacrament, but He is also the freely and lovingly given gift. The two disciples on the road to Emmaus recognized Him in the "breaking of the bread,"[239] another name

---

[237] Matt. 18:20.

[238] Vatican Council II, Constitution on the Sacred Liturgy *Sacrosanctum Concilium* (December 4, 1963), no. 8.

[239] Luke 24:13–35.

for the Holy Eucharist. Do we recognize Him in the celebration of Holy Mass? He assures us that "he who eats my flesh and drinks my blood has eternal life."[240] This is the overwhelming mystery: the Lord uses ordinary and daily things like bread and wine and elevates them to something absolutely sacred, while respecting their very ordinariness. The bread and wine look, feel, taste, and smell like ordinary bread and wine, but at the Words of Consecration they become the means by which we find Him and where we meet Him, in His totality as God and man. We encounter the Lord, and He is our true nourishment in our journey to Heaven.

So, we utter with St. Thomas Aquinas, "O precious and wonderful banquet, that brings us salvation and contains all sweetness! Could anything be of more intrinsic value? ... Here Christ himself, the true God, is set before us as our food. What could be more wonderful than this?"[241]

Penance and Reconciliation

The Sacrament of Baptism forgives all sins, that is, Original Sin and whatever personal sins a person committed before being baptized. But, as we all know from our own personal lives, being baptized does not immunize us to sin. Our frail and sin-prone human nature is not changed after Baptism. So, how are sins committed after Baptism forgiven? Through the Sacrament of Penance and Reconciliation.

This sacrament has been known down the centuries by a number of titles, such as Confession, Forgiveness, Penance, and being Shriven of Sins. The confessing person is called a *penitent*, while the priest who hears the penitent is called a *confessor*. He forgives

---

[240] John 6:54.

[241] From a sermon by St. Thomas Aquinas, *Opusculum 57 in Festo Corporis Christi*, lect. 1–4.

sins in the Person of Christ. No priest or bishop has of himself the power to forgive sins because God alone forgives sins, and God's grace alone makes us turn away from evil and repent.[242] The Lord, through this sacrament, forgives all sins that are confessed during a valid Confession, restores peace between God and the sinner, joins Heaven and earth by the renovated harmony with the Church and within the penitent, and takes away the penalty of Hell in the case of mortal sins. But, purposefully leaving out grave (mortal) sins during a sacramental Confession renders that Confession invalid. However, should we forget to confess any grave sin for some reason,[243] the Confession is valid, but we are still bound to confess forgotten grave sins in a subsequent Confession, once we remember them.

The Lord established the Sacrament of Penance and Reconciliation when He breathed the Holy Spirit upon His apostles and gave them the power to remit sins or hold back forgiveness.[244] The confession of our sins to another person (oral confession) was introduced by St. James.[245] His statement forms part of inspired Sacred Scripture and, consequently, is binding. This sacrament is the *normal* way to procure the absolution of sins, in particular grave sins. Since the Lord Himself bestowed the power to forgive sins on the apostles, and in turn this power is passed on to their

---

[242] Ezek. 36:26–27; Lam. 5:21.

[243] One may forget to confess a sin because he is anxious or distracted, or simply because he has a poor memory. However, that is all the more reason to examine one's conscience thoroughly before entering the confessional. One must also cultivate the virtue of constancy, so that he is not distracted from our spiritual exercises by internal and external stimuli.

[244] John 20:23; see also Matt. 16:19; 18:18; Rev. 1:18; 3:7.

[245] James 5:16.

successors, only bishops and priests may sacramentally validly absolve sins in the name of Jesus Christ. We are forgiven due to God's love and mercy. The Lord's love will melt our icy hearts like butter exposed to a flame.

The celebration of the sacrament consists in four parts or stages, though, in case of danger of death or when one is unconscious, the confessor's absolution suffices as long as the penitent was already repentant, irrespective of whether it is known or not. In ordinary circumstances, the reception of the sacrament consists in the penitent, having done an examination of conscience, being contrite of all sins committed since the last sacramental Confession; next, he confesses all grave sins; then, receives absolution from the confessor; and finally, fulfills the assigned penance.[246]

Our contrition is verbally expressed before receiving absolution. Our contrition must include our resolve to avoid any occasion to sin in the future. The absolution, and hence the sacrament itself, is invalid when we confess but have no intention of amending our life. The confessor need not assign a penance for the Confession to be valid, but these penances are the normal means of lessening the spiritual punishment we merit by sinning, and which will be meted out after death.

In other words, each sin carries a temporal punishment, which is a retribution completed either during our life or after death. When the satisfaction for our sins is not completed before death, then it is brought to conclusion in Purgatory, a state of purification. Since all people sin frequently due to human frailty, this sacrament must be received frequently. Once every two weeks is a good rule of thumb.

[246] See Amos 5:24; Isa. 1:17; Luke 9:23.

The preparation for this sacrament is straightforward. We first prepare ourselves by making an examination of our conscience. This means we confront ourselves with our sins, big and small alike, by examining ourselves since the last valid Confession in order to recognize what was deficient in thought, word, or deed. We must be totally, brutally honest with ourselves—and with God, who knows us in and out, anyway.[247] An honest examination is never comfortable, but it is necessary. As we repent of these sins, we should also resolve to avoid them and any circumstances that might lead to sin.

Next, we go to a confessor to receive the sacrament. We are reminded that we are there not only to confess our sins but to convert. We never surprise God with any sin. Once we have confessed our sins, the confessor might give us some spiritual counsel and encouraging words. He is acting in the Person of Christ and not on his own powers. Only grave sins are required to be confessed, though the Confession of venial sins is recommended.

It should be kept in mind that this sacrament calls the contrite penitent[248] to an authentic conversion.[249] The first conversion involved the call to Baptism, while the second conversion is an ongoing lifelong call that requires adherence more and more to the Lord so that we can join St. Paul when he declares, "Christ … lives in me."[250] Thus, the sacrament involves much more than simply being the ordinary means to have sins forgiven.[251] When we reach the age of reason and are able to distinguish between good and evil, we should start going to Confession, for we are capable of making choices. The Catholic Church commands that

---

[247] Ps. 44:21; 94:11; 139:2; Matt. 9:4; Luke 6:8.

[248] Ps. 51:17; see John 6:44; 12:32; 1 John 4:10.

[249] Mark 1:15.

[250] Gal. 2:20.

[251] See Vatican Council II, *Lumen Gentium*, no. 8, §3.

we go to Confession at least once a year. Furthermore, if we have committed a grave sin, we should express our sorrow to God and go to Confession as soon as possible. We may not receive Holy Eucharist before being sacramentally absolved of any mortal sin.

Perhaps one might ask: What sins should be confessed? The Church distinguishes between two kinds of sin: grave and venial.

There are three conditions that must be present concurrently in order to commit a grave sin. First, the matter must be objectively grave, for example, lying under oath. Second, the person committing it must be aware that the matter is grave. And third, the individual must commit the sin in a willful manner. The penalty for committing a grave sin is eternal damnation. The penalty is removed when a grave sin is absolved at Confession.

The other kind of sin is called *venial* because by its nature it does not sever one's relationship with God, though it harms and weakens it. Venial sins can be forgiven by a simple act of contrition. However, everyone who commits venial sin should still confess them. Though venial sins do not merit that the sinner goes to Hell, there is still satisfaction to be made for them — if not in this life, then in Purgatory.

No sin, no matter how grave, is beyond the reach of God's mercy and forgiveness. Granted, confessing our sins may be a very embarrassing and anxious experience. This might be due to focusing ourselves on the enormity of our sins rather than primarily focusing on the infinite mercy of a loving God. Indeed, Confession exists so God can take our burdens away from us. We should keep in mind what the inspired Psalmist declared centuries ago: "The LORD is merciful and gracious, slow to anger and abounding in steadfast love."[252] We should keep present the calling of St. Matthew the

---

[252] Ps. 103:8.

apostle, a tax collector—one deemed by pious Jews a great sinner and a collaborator with their Roman enemies. St. Bede the Venerable (ca. 673–735) wrote: "Jesus saw Matthew, not merely in the usual sense, but more significantly with His merciful understanding of men. He saw the tax collector and, because He saw him through the eyes of mercy and chose him, He said to him: *Follow me.* This following meant imitating the pattern of His life—not just walking after Him."[253]

Anointing of the Sick

Some people pour millions of dollars into medical procedures and pseudo-scientific practices designed to escape the process of aging and even death itself. Yet, each living thing will eventually return to the dust from which it was created. We begin dying the moment we are conceived. What happens between that moment and the moment of death is called life on earth.

Since the Lord wants to be with us especially when we are not well, He established the Sacrament of the Anointing of the Sick. It confers a special sacramental grace on its recipient. The Lord alluded to this sacrament when He sent the twelve apostles on a mission to preach repentance. It was during this mission that they anointed sick people with oil, and many were healed.[254] After His Ascension, the apostle James, reflecting on the Lord's directives, recommended the calling of the Church elders to anoint a sick person in the name of the Lord and pray over the individual.[255] The priests and bishops of the Church have been anointing and praying over the sick since that time.

---

[253] St. Bede the Venerable, *Homily 21.*
[254] Mark 6:7–13.
[255] James 5:14–16.

No one escapes some shade of suffering. Our personal travails should be joined to the sufferings of the Lord,[256] instead of becoming self-absorbed. The sacrament provides us with an opportunity of acquiring a Christ-oriented mindset. This attitude also contributes toward the holiness of the Church[257] and, at times, even physical and mental healing.

Over the years, the Catholic Church has established a specific way and a standard set of words to be used during the administration of this sacrament. The essential elements of the sacrament have never changed. They are (1) the anointing with holy oil while (2) praying using the approved words, and (3) the absolution of sins. A validly ordained priest or bishop is the only administrator of this sacrament because it involves the sacramental absolution of sins. This sacrament reflects the fact that Jesus not only healed the physically sick but also forgave their sins.[258] Accordingly, He healed the whole person.[259] The Church recommends that whenever possible, the Anointing of the Sick should include the Sacrament of Penance and Reconciliation, as well as Holy Communion.

Originally, the sacrament was associated with approaching death, giving it the name of *Extreme Unction*. However, the Second Vatican Council changed the name to the *Sacrament of the Anointing of the Sick*,[260] and subsequently Pope St. Paul VI issued an apostolic constitution that introduced changes in the administration of the sacrament, one of which allowed it to be administered also when a person is seriously ill, or when one's physical condition worsens,

---

[256] Isa. 53:4; Matt. 8:17.

[257] Vatican Council II, *Lumen Gentium*, no. 11, §2.

[258] Mark 2:5–12.

[259] Mark 2:17.

[260] Vatican Council II, *Sacrosanctum Concilium*, no. 73.

or due to old age. Thus, we may receive the sacrament a number of times during our lifetime.[261]

The aim of this sacrament pertains to our whole person, body and soul. It aims at strengthening us during some kind of illness and restoring our spiritual health through the absolution of our sins. It is also recommended that we ask for the sacrament prior to a serious surgery. The sacrament may be celebrated simultaneously for a group of people.

The sick person, after the laying on of hands by the priest, is anointed on the forehead and on the hands with the blessed oil of the sick, while the priest pronounces the Church-approved formula for anointing. There are times when physical healing also occurs. However, the underlying disposition is that God's will be done, as the sick person seeks to join his or her sufferings to those of the Lord.

In past centuries, Catholics often were afraid to call the priest to administer the sacrament because it was associated with imminent death. They thought that, unless someone is clearly in his final hours, the priest should not be bothered. Some still hold on to this mentality. It takes time, patience, and instruction to educate Catholics to realize that this sacrament should not be put off until someone is on the verge of death.

Before one receives the sacrament, there are a number of steps that should be taken—unless, of course, one is too sick to do so. We should prepare ourselves to receive the sacrament with faith and trust in the Lord's goodness and mercy. Whenever possible, other persons should be present and participate in prayers during the celebration of the sacrament. We should receive the sacrament of Penance and Reconciliation without the presence of

---

[261] Pope Paul VI, Apostolic Constitution on the Sacrament of Anointing of the Sick *Sacram Unctione Infirmorum* (November 30, 1972).

third parties. We should receive Holy Communion—which, when received for the last time, as part of the sacrament of Anointing, is known as *Viaticum*. Thus, the faithful are able to participate in the celebration of this sacrament. However, in the case of imminent death, and especially when the sick person is either incoherent or unconscious, the priest uses a very brief formula for the anointing and gives absolution, adding to it a plenary indulgence.

This sacrament is always associated with the Passion, death, and Resurrection of the Lord. The grace of this sacrament unites us with the sufferings of the Lord, for our own good and that of the Church. It gives us strength, inner peace, and courage to endure suffering in a Christian way. It forgives our sins if we are unable to receive the Sacrament of Penance and Reconciliation. It seeks healing of mind and body if this is in accordance with God's will. It prepares us for eternal life.

An article written by Mary Jordan and Kevin Sullivan on September 17, 2021, in the *Washington Post* had the headline "Tens of Thousands Die Each Year in the United States and No One Claims Their Bodies." The article stated that these people are either abandoned by their survivors, usually for reasons of financial hardship, or because the deceased had lost contact with their families. This deplorable fact may be true on the external level. But a person never dies alone. In truth, the Lord, accompanied by Our Lady, St. Joseph, the community of saints, and the angels, is present at the moment of every human person's death, when the lowering of the curtain of time over our human life takes place. We are never alone, even if no other human being is present at our side.

Lord, You are the one who "gives to all men life and breath and everything."[262] Lord, we ask for healing if it is Your will.

---

[262] Acts 17:25.

Marriage

As we mature, we make a lot of choices that will influence the rest our lives. One of these choices is that of a lifelong commitment. However, there are only two such commitments that are recognized as sacraments: Marriage and priesthood. The other kinds of commitments are most honorable and make a pronounced difference in the life of the Church and society at large. These are the vocation to the religious life, wherein public vows or promises are assumed; to hermitical life; or to consecrated virginity. Naturally, a priest in the Western (Latin) Church, with some exceptions, is called to be celibate. All those who belong to religious orders — whether as nuns, brothers, or priests — are also called to celibacy, without exception.

Unlike the Old Testament Levites, whose priesthood was handed down from father to son, the Levites of the New Testament have no natural progeny and they must pray, along with the entire Church, to have holy and dedicated successors, bound to them by ordination.

The largest part of the Church is comprised of laypeople, and the majority of laypeople are married or will someday be married. The Church needs the laity. One day, the witty St. John Henry (Cardinal) Newman (1801–1890), who converted from Anglicanism, was asked about the laity in the Catholic Church. He responded that the Church would look foolish without the laity.[263] This is a verifiable fact. This saint, way ahead of his time, wrote about the duty of every adult Catholic layperson:

> You must not hide your talent in a napkin, or your light under a bushel. I want a laity, not arrogant, not rash in

---

[263] St. John Henry Newman, *On Consulting the Faithful in Matters of Doctrine*, pp. 28–29.

speech, not disputatious, but men and women who know their religion, who enter into it, who know just where they stand, who know what they hold and what they do not, who know their creed so well that they can give an account of it, who know so much of history that they can defend it. I want an intelligent and well-instructed laity.... I wish you to enlarge your knowledge, to cultivate your reason, to get an insight into the relation of truth, to learn to view things as they are, to understand how faith and reason stand to each other, what are the bases and principles of Catholicism.

The Sacrament of Marriage has its roots in the book of Genesis.[264] Despite many determinations of our culture and secular legislation to redefine nature's state of things and natural law, basing arguments on individual rights, a true and authentic marriage must be always between a man and a woman. Jesus elevated Marriage from a natural bond to a sacrament[265] when He quoted the Old Testament on this subject and condemned divorce.[266] The prophet Malachi had declared, "So take heed to yourselves, and let none be faithless to the wife of his youth. For I hate divorce, says the LORD the God of Israel."[267] Later, St. Paul elaborated on this matter in Ephesians[268] and 1 Corinthians.[269] The sacrament is present between two baptized persons, bride and groom, since the reception of Baptism enables us to receive the other sacraments.

---

[264] Gen. 2:24.
[265] Vatican Council II, Pastoral Constitution on the Church in the Modern World *Gaudium et Spes* (December 7, 1965), no. 48, §1.
[266] Matt. 19:1-9; Mark 10:2-12.
[267] Mal. 2:15-16.
[268] Eph. 5:22-23.
[269] 1 Cor. 7:10-16.

Otherwise, marriage between a baptized and a non-baptized or two unbaptized persons remains a natural bond that can be dissolved by the competent Church authority so as to enable one to enter into a sacramental union.

The ministers of the Sacrament of Marriage are the bride and the groom themselves. The ceremony must take place in the presence of two alert witnesses who have reached the age of reason. A priest or deacon receives the spouses' individual consent in the name of the Church,[270] since marriage is a public state of life in the Church. The presence of these three persons is essential for the validity of the sacrament. There are a number of formulas approved by the Church for the exchange of the marriage vows. When the marrying couple validly exchanges their marriage vows, they become united "as one" in God's eyes[271] and are publicly and canonically recognized as a married couple.

Just as the Church may not recognize a marriage between siblings, she, independent of civil legislation, does not recognize same-sex marriage.

Marriage is a holy covenant for life and lasts as long as both spouses are still alive. In consenting to marry in the Church, the baptized couple declares that the sacrament they are celebrating is indissoluble and requires exclusive fidelity and openness to have children. When either marriage partner is sterile for some reason,[272] the openness to children is moot and does not affect the

---

[270] The Eastern Catholic Churches prohibit a deacon to validly conduct a marriage.

[271] Matt. 19:6.

[272] Examples of this are when a man is sterile or a woman is past child-bearing years. Sterility is radically different from impotence, and the presence of the latter at the time of Marriage renders the union null and void.

validity of marital consent. A valid, consummated union between two baptized persons can never be dissolved by any earthly power, not even the pope.

The Church teaches that a sacramental Marriage is a covenant between a man and a woman, equal in dignity, whereby the couple establishes a lifelong partnership that is ordered by its very nature to the good of the spouses and the procreation and education of children. It should be remembered that this sacrament is aimed at the salvation of the spouses and their children. The spouses are already consecrated by virtue of their Baptism and Confirmation. When they celebrate the Sacrament of Marriage, they are fortified by the grace of the sacrament to fulfill their duties as spouses and parents in their dignity as a married couple. By its very nature, God Himself is the author of Marriage and instilled the vocation of Marriage into the very nature of man and woman. God blessed them and directed them to be fruitful by having offspring.[273] Just as Jesus Christ entered into an unbreakable covenant with the Church, His bride,[274] so, too, when a couple marries validly, it establishes an unbreakable covenant between the spouses and reflects the covenant between Christ and His Church. In reflecting this Christ-Church unbreakable bond, the marrying couple enters into an intimate communion of life and love. Just as the Lord gives Himself completely to His Bride and vice versa, so too, spouses are to give themselves to one another as they struggle to overcome self-centeredness and all that this entails. Thus, though the Sacrament of Marriage is initiated at the wedding ceremony, it is an ongoing, daily process as the couple grows together in its sacred marital commitment and mirrors the union between Christ and His Bride, the Church.

[273] Gen. 1:22, 28.
[274] 1 Cor. 7:39; Eph. 5:31-32.

The bride and the groom must both be willing to enter the union and be capable of assuming the rights and responsibilities thereof. A paralyzed person might be willing to run, but cannot do so because he or she is incapacitated. In a similar fashion, a person contracting Marriage must be knowledgeable and willing not only to take on the responsibilities and rights of marrying but also capable of carrying them out. These acts must be assumed in an exclusive and lifelong marital relationship. Thus, unity, indissolubility, and openness to children are essential to Marriage.

The family home is called a *domestic church*.[275] The home of a married couple is a place where its members not only live according to their Christian vocation, but is also a place that provides education to their children in Christian lifestyle and values. It is a dynamic place where the Lord is present and very involved in the household. Alas, many married couples are not aware of the Lord's presence and involvement in their marriage and, thus, fail to call on Him through regular praying.

The Church puts great importance on the Lord's presence at the Wedding at Cana in Galilee.[276] His presence affirmed the goodness of Marriage and proclaimed that henceforth He will be present in a marital union. Once the Lord embarked on His public ministry, He plainly spoke of the original meaning of Marriage as a union established by God Himself and affirmed that no human power can put this aside, even though Moses had given permission for a divorce due to man's hardness of heart.[277] Afterward, St. Paul reemphasized this teaching in his writings.[278] Our current society

---

[275] Vatican Council II, *Lumen Gentium*, no. 11.
[276] John 2:1–11.
[277] Matt. 19:6–8.
[278] Eph. 5:25–26, 31–32; Rom. 7:2–3.

persistently assails the divine affirmation of marital indissolubility. This is nothing new in the history of the Church. This offense produces nothing but broken families, calumnies based on hurt and deep resentment, emotional and physical abuse between the spouses, severe and sometimes long-lasting damage to the children, unwillingness to acknowledge grave mistakes, and so forth. It certainly does not reflect the love that Christ, the Groom, has for His Church, the Bride—a love that the spouses had originally promised to each other and to the faith community at large on their wedding day. Many a time, children, the concrete expression of the couple's mutual love, become the subject of a tug-of-war between the spouses, producing much insecurity, confusion, and anxiety. Many a time, the separated or divorced spouses are unwilling to step back and realize the harm that they are inflicting. They are too caught up in themselves. Of course, this does not apply to every separated or divorced couple, but it is not uncommon.

When we analyze what takes place in the celebration of a sacramental Marriage, we discover that there are three persons in the Marriage: the husband, the wife, and the Lord. Indeed, a sacramental Marriage in ancient times was called being *married in the Lord*. It is a vocation that requires great sacrifices through the emptying of each spouse's self so as to become fully dedicated to God, to the other spouse, and to their children. This enriches the proper family and the Church at large. The Lord supplies the spouses with the special graces of this sacrament. As already stated, many couples forget to call on the Lord to assist them to grow in their marriage. The Lord wants to be really involved in their marriage. Pope Francis has said, "The image of God is the married couple: the man and the woman; not only the man, not only the woman, but both of them together. This is the image of God: love, God's covenant with us is represented in that covenant between man and woman. And this is very beautiful!"[279] A couple of years later, he said the following: "Many of you are married, others are about to get married; remember these three words, which have helped so much in married life: 'may I?,' 'thank you,' and 'I'm sorry.' "[280]

Holy Orders

The Lord, in order to remain ever present in His Church, established the Sacrament of Holy Orders. This sacrament, therefore, is always associated with Holy Eucharist, where His *Real Presence* exists on earth. There can be no Holy Eucharist without a priest, and if there is no Holy Eucharist, priestly ministry is futile.

For some time now, the Church has been in dire need of priests. The seeds of vocations to the priesthood and to the religious life are usually planted within the sanctuary of our respective homes. Likewise, a family can unfortunately stamp out the first seedlings of a vocation. No boy wishes to disappoint his parents by becoming a priest when the family is constantly criticizing priests. Some criticism is well founded, especially during this era of scandal, but there should be a limit to criticism. Parents should warn their children about bad priests, but also go out of their way to praise good ones.

The Church does not need a superabundance of priests. She is in need of *holy* priests, no matter how small or large in number. So, let us pray every day for holy priests, for, as the Lord stated, "The harvest is plentiful, but the laborers are few; pray therefore the Lord of the harvest to send out laborers into his harvest."[281]

---

[279] Pope Francis, General Audience (April 2, 2014).
[280] Pope Francis, Greeting to the Faithful, Archbishop's House, Krakow, Poland (July 28, 2016).
[281] Matt. 9:37–38.

I believe that, especially during these unsettling times, good priests are voices crying out in the wilderness of our self-enamored society: "Prepare the way of the Lord; go back to the way of the Lord; walk the way of the Lord." The priest is the vehicle for Christ's power: when he pronounces the Words of Consecration, God comes down from Heaven. The priest is the instrument through which the Great Physician touches the penitent soul and heals it, spiritually and physically. However, no one has a "right" to receive Holy Orders. That calling is a gift, which God gives to whomever He chooses. This is why bishops are ultimately responsible for discerning the authenticity of a person's calling to Holy Orders.

The Sacrament of Holy Orders has three degrees or phases: deacon, priest, and bishop. All three require sacred ordination. As is in the case of Baptism and Confirmation, this sacrament marks the recipient's soul for eternity.[282]

The Lord Himself established these orders of priest and bishop when He called and appointed the twelve apostles as priests and bishops of the new dispensation.[283] Because the Lord entrusted the sacraments to His Church, the apostles added the order of deacon to meet the needs of the non-Hebrew Christians at that time.[284] Holy Orders binds the ordained minister to the mission that the Lord originally entrusted to His apostles and their successors in the office of bishop, as individuals and as a body. Christ endowed the apostles with a very special outpouring of the Holy Spirit so that they would be able to fulfill this lofty mission. The apostles appointed their own successors who, in turn, appointed their successors. This has been going on down

---

[282] Ps. 110:4; Heb. 5:6; 7:17.
[283] Matt. 10:1–4; Mark 3:13–19; Luke 6:12–16.
[284] Acts 6:6; 1 Tim. 4:14; 5:22; 2 Tim. 1:6.

to our times in an unbroken chain and is called the *apostolic succession*.

A civil body in ancient Rome, especially a governing one, was called an *ordo* (in English "order"). The induction into the body was called *ordinatio* (in English "ordination"). The Church adopted the term *ordo* to her hierarchy, calling it *Holy Orders*. The act of being incorporated into this body is called *sacred ordination*. The integration of a person into this body takes place at the ordination of the candidate within a liturgical celebration. It involves the laying on of hands and, in the case of bishops and priests, anointing the person with the sacred chrism oil. There is no anointing during the ordination of a deacon, whether he is ordained as a *transitional* deacon on the way to the priesthood or as a *permanent* deacon. The priest's hands are anointed, however, while the crown of the head is anointed in the case of a new bishop. The ordination of the candidate bestows upon him the gift of the Holy Spirit, which enables him to exercise a sacred power in the Church that has its source in Jesus Christ the High Priest.[285] Bishops alone may validly ordain other bishops, priests, and deacons.

Baptism makes all of us members of what is known as the *universal priesthood*. This mission is reinforced by the reception of the Sacrament of Confirmation. However, the Sacrament of Holy Orders is apart and distinct in nature and character from the universal priesthood. When one receives the Sacrament of Holy Orders, they become capable of acting *in Persona* (in the Person of) Jesus Christ—the sole Priest of the New Covenant—by, for instance, consecrating the Eucharist or forgiving sins.

No one is born a priest or bishop. Each priest is called from those who are members of the universal priesthood. Since

---

[285] Heb. 4:14-15; 6:20; 7:26.

Jesus Christ is the one and only mediator between God and all people,[286] there is no ministerial priesthood without the high priesthood of Jesus Christ.[287] Ordination to the priesthood bestows the sacred power of Christ upon the priest. The Church teaches that the fullness of the Sacrament of Holy Orders is bestowed by episcopal consecration and that episcopacy enjoys the summit of sacred ministry.[288] The consecration to the episcopacy confers upon the new bishop the mission to sanctify, to teach, and to govern that section of the People of God entrusted to his care and service. The special grace of the Holy Spirit belonging to this sacrament constitutes bishops as the true and authentic teachers of the Faith and local shepherds of God's flock. A bishop is marked with a sacred character that enables him to act as the eminent and visible representative of Christ to the local community of faith (known as a *diocese*) that is entrusted to his episcopal mission.

Like all priests, the bishop acts in the Person of Christ while celebrating the sacraments, though he does not cease to be like other frail human beings, prone to sin. Thus, the exercise of this sacred authority must imitate Christ, who is the humble servant of all people.[289] The Holy Spirit ensures the fruit of grace from the sacrament, irrespective of a minister's personal spiritual status. The way the priest and the bishop carry out servanthood to the faithful should always reflect their love for Christ.[290]

---

[286] 1 Tim. 2:5.

[287] Heb. 8:4.

[288] Vatican Council II, *Lumen Gentium*, no. 21, §2.

[289] Mark 10:43–45; 1 Pet. 5:3.

[290] John 21:15–17; see Vatican Council II, Decree on the Ministry and Life of Priests *Presbyterorum Ordinis* (December 7, 1965), nos. 3, 12.

Just as God established the Jewish nation as priests, Jesus Christ established the Church as a priestly community.[291] The Church sees an anticipation of the priesthood of Jesus Christ and the priests of the New Covenant in the priesthood of Aaron and the hereditary priesthood of the Levites, adding also that of the ageless (non-Jewish) high priest Melchizedek.[292] Jesus Christ is the one and only true High Priest, and His one priesthood is made present through the ministerial priesthood of the New Covenant. These priests, as already stated, act *in Persona Christi* as His ministers.

A bishop's consecration inducts him into a body known as the College of Bishops, which is the entire body of Catholic bishops who are in communion with one another, and individually and as a body in communion with the Bishop of Rome, the pope, who serves as the Head of the Church, as well as the supreme visible bond of communion among all the dioceses[293] and their equivalent. This is called *collegiality*. Each bishop is the vicar of Christ to his proper diocese while, at the same time, due to collegiality, is also responsible with all the other bishops for the apostolic mission of the universal Church.

Bishops, through their apostolic succession, share in the Lord's consecration and mission. They, in turn, entrust in a subordinate degree some of their episcopal ministry to priests as their coworkers. This handing over is carried out through the ordination rite of priests, which is enacted by an ordaining bishop.

The relationship between the ministry of priests and bishops is essentially intertwined. The priests' power as ministers derives

---

[291] Rev. 1:6; 5:9–10; 1 Pet. 2:5, 9.

[292] Heb. 5:10; 6:20; Gen. 14:18.

[293] Church law refers to a diocese as a *particular church* (*Code of Canon Law*, can. 373).

from the bishop's ministerial powers, and priests depend on their respective bishops to carry out their ministry. The exercise of their priestly ministry must also take place in unity with their proper bishop. Catholic priests are the Levites of the New Testament.[294] As bride and groom join their right hands to pronounce their marriage vows, so does the ordinand join his own hands and place them between those of the bishop who is ordaining him. He declares his obedience to his bishop and that bishop's lawful successors, as well as selfless service to the Church, his spouse. Through Holy Orders, priests share in the universal mission that Christ entrusted to His apostles and their successors. Priests exercise in a supreme degree their sacred office at the celebration of the sacrifice of Holy Mass, during which they act in the Person of Christ, the Head of the Church.

It has already been stated that only validly ordained bishops many ordain deacons, priests, and other bishops. This is so because Christ personally and specifically chose the apostles and entrusted to them a share in His mission and authority. Thus, only those bishops who enjoy apostolic succession may ordain validly other men to Holy Orders. Since Christ chose only men to form the college of the apostles, the Church is permanently bound to do the same until the Lord's return in glory.[295]

The diaconate belongs to the ministry of service. It is the deacon's mission to help the bishops' and priests' mission of service to God's people. Thus, they are charged to assist during the celebration of Holy Mass, distribute Holy Communion, officiate at marriages, proclaim and preach the Gospel, preside at funerals,

---

[294] Heb. 5:1-10; 7:24; 9:11-28.

[295] John Paul II, Apostolic Letter on Reserving Priestly Ordination to Men Alone *Ordinatio Sacerdotalis* (May 24, 1994).

give benediction with the Blessed Sacrament, and provide ministries of charity.

The Lord said through the prophet Isaiah: "Every one who thirsts, come to the waters."[296] Lord, we are thirsty for holy ordained ministers. We ask You to quench our thirst.

---

[296] Isa. 55:1.

6

The Old Testament: Our Spiritual Heritage

Genuine Reporting

Our respective situations in life are very diverse. Yet one thing is constant: we must rely on the grace of God, the movement of the Holy Spirit within our personal lives and hearts, of being held by the hand by our Blessed Mother, who says to each of us: "Come with me to meet my Son, your Brother who will refresh you by giving you living waters."[297] Too many times, it seems we Catholics have it all wrong when it comes to understanding how God speaks. We usually think of the Lord appearing to someone and speaking to them directly, as in a vision or apparition. We think of the Lord's appearance to His disciples in the Upper Room, or of St. Paul's experience on the road to Emmaus. We might think of Jesus speaking during a vision to people like St. Francis of Assisi, St. Juliana of Liege, St. Catherine of Siena, St. Teresa of Ávila, St. Margaret Mary Alacoque, St. Veronica Giuliani, St. Gemma Galgani, St. Padre Pio, St. Faustina Kowalska, and Bl. Anne Catherine

---

[297] See John 7:38-39.

Emmerich. But Jesus speaks to us individually all the time. The question is, do we listen?

The Church declares that Sacred Scripture is the Word of God, the voice of God. Thus, every time a part of Sacred Scripture is read or proclaimed, Jesus is speaking to us. Jesus also speaks to us through the voice of the Teaching Church. We should constantly be attentive, because Jesus' voice is that of the one who proclaims Sacred Scripture and the Church's authoritative teachings. We should listen prayerfully and attentively, for the Lord declares, "My sheep hear my voice, I know them, and they follow me."[298] The seductive voices of the world are louder than the soothing voice of the Lord. So, it is rather easy to not hear the Lord speaking to us in the humdrum and the cacophonies of daily life.

So much of that cacophony comes from the media. Objective and accurate reporting is necessary for the common good, and yet members of the press have other priorities. They decide which facts to disclose to the public, and how to spin those facts, in service to an ideological agenda. Often, they simply lie to us! Worst of all, they do so in a way calculated to inspire fear and anger in the public.

I am troubled when I read such headings as "Important News You Missed This Weekend" and "Everything That You Need to Know Today." The news items might be important to the reporters, but not to me. The press treats us like small children—as if we don't know what's good for ourselves!

I find something very interesting when comparing the way some reported news of the heinous crime of clergy abuse of minors, especially Catholic clergy, and of police abuse of innocent people. It goes without saying that both crimes must be always condemned. Perpetrators must be prosecuted and punished for their repulsive

---

[298] John 10:27; see also John 10:4.

crimes. Still, reports continue to be presented in such a way that all Catholic clergy and all police officers are now suspect. Forget the very dedicated clergy who spend their lives ministering to all sorts of people, Catholic and not, in the name of the Lord. (And forget those of non-Catholic establishments and institutions who sexually abuse innocent victims!)

Likewise, the dedicated work of honest law enforcement officers—who are also in the great majority, as is the case with Catholic clergy—is left out when reporting police abuse and atrocities. It is all lopsided. The impression is given that all police officers are guilty. Some reporters, or even an entire staff of a media outlet, have decided that honest clergy and law enforcement officers are not worth their time or consideration. Are these newspersons the new unaccountable tyrants? They expect us to suspend our intelligence and instead allow them control over our judgment and feelings.

The above reminds me of an incident in the Old Testament when its version of newscasters decided to twist their report. The Old Testament book of Numbers[299] relates how Moses, following divine instructions, sent surveyors to evaluate the Promised Land (Canaan) and report their findings back to him. The Bible tells us, "They brought to the people of Israel an evil report of the land."[300] They reported nothing about the richness of the land but had plenty to say about the land that "devours its inhabitants" and the resident "men of great stature" who made them look like "grasshoppers." The Israelites became very frightened, wanted to replace Moses and select a new leader, and wanted to return to Egypt, the land where they had been oppressed and enslaved. The people had forgotten God's promises, had forgotten that God had

---

[299] Num. 13–14.
[300] Num. 13:32.

set them free from slavery, had forgotten the parting of the Red Sea, had forgotten the manna and the quail that God had given them as food during the previous forty years. In other words, the reports were distorted, and the reporters were so successful in manipulating people's emotions that an entire nation lost its trust in their loving, compassionate, merciful, and faithful God and His love for them. The report of this incident might be the first written account of manipulated news!

Pope Francis wrote in 2020: "We need media that can help people, especially the young, to distinguish good from evil, to develop sound judgments based on a clear and unbiased presentation of the facts, and to understand the importance of working for justice, social concord and respect for our common home. We need men and women of conviction who protect communication from all that would distort it or bend it to other purposes."[301] Some months later, while meeting with the Vatican journalists on May 24, 2021, he prayed: "Lord, teach us to come out of ourselves, and to set out in search of the truth. Teach us to go and see, teach us to listen, not to cultivate prejudices, not to draw hasty conclusions."[302]

I invite all of us to open our hearts and minds to God so that our souls may be sanctified by God's grace. The authentic message of the Old Testament should assist us in pinning down our fears, frustrations, anxieties, profound questions, and perhaps a crisis in our trust of God. The Psalmist cried out: "We are slain all the day long.... Rouse thyself! Why sleepest thou, O Lord?... Rise up, come to our help!"[303] But also, hear God and then affirm with the inspired

---

[301] Pope Francis, Message to the Catholic Media Conference (June 30, 2020).

[302] Pope Francis, Meeting with Vatican Journalists (May 24, 2021).

[303] Ps. 44:22–26.

Psalmist, who speaks on God's behalf: "You are my son, today I have begotten you,"[304] and, "With the LORD on my side I do not fear."[305]

What Is Sacred Scripture?

We are heirs of Sacred Scripture in its entirety. Indeed, God gave these Scriptures to the Church as part of her divine dowry.

But what is Sacred Scripture? Simply put, it is the Word of God communicated in human language. When He speaks to us, He takes great pains to make Himself understood. This dual aspect of the Bible is very important in trying to understand these sacred writings. Furthermore, for a Christian, the Old and New Testaments are one unit that provides us an account of the promises made to the world via the Jewish people (Old Testament)—promises that are fulfilled in Jesus Christ (New Testament).

We need to listen carefully so as to come to know what God is telling us, especially during these very stressful times, when it is rather easy to panic or to feel insignificant or simply ignored.

History repeats itself. Many prophets in the Old Testament called their fellow countrymen to reform and repent and go back to their senses. Then, after the prophets were ignored and the people experienced lots of sufferings and rejection, they were utterly surprised with the catastrophes that followed! God created all of us, but some choose to travel their path and do it their way. We may not blame God for this.

The Bible is the Word of God because God Himself speaks to us in these sacred writings. He is the ultimate Author. He is the one in whom the communication finds its origins. On the other hand, because God wants to converse with human beings, God uses

---

[304] Ps. 2:7.
[305] Ps. 118:6.

the means of human language and, at times, even the messenger's gestures, to get across His message, which has never changed: I am madly in love with you, frail human being.

God's communication comes to us through human beings who, just like every one of us, are limited and conditioned by their respective personal, social, psychological, cultural, and historical settings and situations, in other words, by their own life stories. What does one do when an entire people is illiterate, as was the case with the Jews during most of the Old Testament times? One speaks to them at their level. Thus, the Old Testament presents God the Father in anthropomorphic language—that is, as if He is a human being with changing moods and strong passions, though every Jew knew that God is pure spirit, lacks gender, and, unlike a human being or an idol, is not physically restricted by time or space.

Perhaps another question frequently asked about the contents of the Bible is: "Is it historically accurate?" The answer to this question requires mental agility. While everything in the Bible is true, the kinds of *truth* it is trying to express are not generally the ones you find in history or science textbooks. Biblical history is unlike our modern understanding of history, which demands reporting facts with accuracy and impartiality of judgment. Biblical history, with some noted exceptions, is less concerned with objectively reporting in precise detail all the facts regarding a situation or event and is more concerned with drawing out the *meaning* of those historical facts as they fall within the overall plan of God's salvation of humanity. It looks at how the hand of God guides human history, particularly that of the Old Testament Jews. Its purpose is to disclose the action of the living and loving God in human affairs. In other words, it is *sacred history*.

When we treat the Bible as a textbook in the modern sense, denying any development in the understanding of its contents, we end up with a very subjective and flawed interpretation. This stance entails many frustrations because the Bible contains passages that seem to contradict one another. Of course, when we understand that the Scriptures are trying to illuminate deeper truths—and when we read these passages in light of the Church's infallible Magisterium—the contradictions disappear!

All of the aforementioned indicates how important it is for us to keep in mind the divine and human elements in the Bible. God speaks to us through fellow human beings whom He specifically selected for that purpose. Thus, we have to understand the human writer in order to understand what God is revealing to us in Sacred Scripture. Consequently, our understanding of what is being revealed depends on how much we understand the human author. This is why the role of the teaching authority in the Catholic Church becomes paramount, for it is a gift that the Holy Spirit has bestowed on her. One does not have to be a biblical scholar or a theologian to read Sacred Scripture, but one has to know the teachings of the Church to understand and correctly interpret the Sacred Book. The Church invites every one of her members to read, study, and pray the Bible frequently. In order to do so, we must know what the Church teaches for the correct interpretation and understanding of the Word of God. It is only then that we can join the Psalmist and say, "[Lord,] Thy word is a lamp to my feet and a light to my path,"[306] for "with thee is the fountain of life; in thy light do we see light."[307]

When historical events are approached as being the acts of a providential God, then it is *sacred history*. The Lord provides us with time. It is called our personal lives. We can make that time

[306] Ps. 119:105.
[307] Ps. 36:9.

our own, and focus on ourselves—or we can make that time God's time to us, and so see how the Lord acts in our personal lives.

Catholics and the Old Testament

The great Doctor of the Church, St. Augustine (AD 354-430), recalls at the beginning of chapter 12 of book 8 in his *Confessions* that, while visiting his friend Alypius in Milan in AD 386, he heard a child's voice repeating the words, "Pick it up and read it. Pick it up and read it." He felt compelled to open Sacred Scripture and began reading. It was the first step in his conversion to the Catholic Faith. He was eventually baptized by St. Ambrose (AD 340-397) during the Easter Vigil on April 24, AD 387, along with his son Adeodatus and his friend Alypius.

The Sacred Book changed Augustine's life, thereby providing the Church with one of its most famous Doctors and geniuses, who became a great spiritual and theological influence in the Church since his lifetime and down to our own days.

Later, in the same autobiographical work, he wrote, "You have made us for yourself, Lord, and our hearts are restless until they rest in you."[308] We, repentant and forgiven sinners in the company of St. Augustine, seek the same rest or stillness in God when we are troubled. We especially do so in a time of great crisis, such as the one we find ourselves in now.

God's grace acts through Sacred Scripture to transform faithful believers into pilgrims who walk in the company of saints and sinners, a people whose earthly members, though spiritually frail, at times stagger and limp, at other times walk, and still at other times run toward the eternal embrace of God, awaiting the final curtain to come down over our eyes and never go up again. May

---

[308] St. Augustine, *Confessions*, bk. 1:2.

we speed forward to eternal light and find repose in the Lord's everlasting peace! Meanwhile, we are nourished by Holy Eucharist and the Word of God, cleansed by Baptism and sacramental Reconciliation, vested by the gifts of the Holy Spirit, shielded from evil by guardian angels, and heartened by Our Lady and the saints.

I suggest that the major themes in the Old Testament remain valid today as humanity finds itself in an extraordinary predicament. We are invited to "open and read" the Word of God as presented in the time of preparation for the arrival of the Lord as we, too, live in preparation in joyful hope for His return in glory. As stated elsewhere, we should read the Bible frequently as members of the Catholic Church.

The first ecumenical council in the history of the Catholic Church was the Council of Jerusalem around AD 50.[309] Twenty more ecumenical councils followed over the next two thousand years. We may be familiar with some of their names, for example Nicaea I in 325, Constantinople I in 381, Ephesus in 431, Trent from 1545 to 1563, and Vatican I from 1869 to 1870. The last ecumenical council to date was Vatican II from 1962 to 1965.

One of the major problems that the Church encountered since the Middle Ages came when a person began interpreting Sacred Scripture on his or her own power, regardless or perhaps ignorant of the teachings of the Church, including the infallible teachings of the ecumenical councils as to that date. This led Rome to discourage lay Catholics from reading Sacred Scripture for fear that it might lead into heresy and encourage others to share those views.

We should keep in mind that, for most of Church history, the greatest part of the laity was illiterate. Thus, the literate person wielded a great deal of power in his community. It was especially

---

[309] Acts 15.

easy for heretics to spread their errors to the illiterate, who were unable to "check the sources" (i.e., the Scriptures).

But the Church's words of caution were widely ignored, leading to a concatenation of circumstances culminating in the Protestant Reformation of the sixteenth century.

Martin Luther, of course, was the first leader of the Reformation. One of his first acts was to translate the Bible into German, making it accessible to those who could read. Those who abandoned the Catholic Church set up their own churches. When some controversy arose in interpreting Sacred Scripture, the dissenting group split up and formed its own independent church. The dissent continues today, with countless non-Catholic churches found across the world.

The passage of time saw the majority of people living in Western civilization become educated and literate. These days, laymen are not only able to read Sacred Scripture, but also make significant contributions to Catholic scriptural scholarship because they are very well versed in the teachings of the Church. Thus, people do not have to rely exclusively on the expertise of one person, and they can no longer be as easily misled.

The Second Vatican Council asked and encouraged lay Catholics to read part of Sacred Scripture frequently, so as to deepen their relationship with God and with their fellow human beings.[310] This prayerful approach should also lead to a better understanding of what is happening in our personal lives and how to approach personal issues in struggles that arise just by simply being alive. Since Vatican II, popes have frequently asked Catholics to read and pray Sacred Scripture. Most recently, Pope Francis, during his

---

[310] Vatican Council II, Dogmatic Constitution on Divine Revelation *Dei Verbum* (November 18, 1965), no. 25.

general audience on Ash Wednesday 2020, right before the beginning of the Covid-19 pandemic, said, "It is the right time to turn off the television and open the Bible. It is the time to disconnect from cellphones and connect ourselves to the Gospel."[311] Little did he and the rest of us suspect at the time that we soon would be given plenty of opportunity to do so because of the lockdowns! The previous month, during his homily at Holy Mass inside St. Peter's Basilica to mark the newly established Sunday of the Word of God, the Holy Father stated that "to follow Jesus, mere good works are not enough; we have to listen daily to his call. He, who alone knows us and who loves us fully, leads us to push out into the deep of life.... That is why we need his word: so that we can hear, amid the thousands of other words in our daily lives, that one word that speaks to us not about things, but about life."[312]

Sacred Scripture is the narrative of a love story between an ever-faithful God and a frequently rebellious and unfaithful humanity—the latter comprising not only the ancient Jews but also the first Christians. These rebellious Christians are referred to in the Letters of St. Paul[313] and St. John.[314] As we can see, the Church has always had to deal with doctrinal controversies! However, God is also in love with all who belong to other faiths or even to no official faith because He creates every human being in His image and likeness. The Lord, out of love for humanity, came down from Heaven and wants to establish a personal relationship with every human being. We should understand that although we are

---

[311] Pope Francis, General Audience (February 26, 2020).

[312] Pope Francis, Homily on Sunday of the Word of God (January 26, 2020).

[313] Rom. 16:17; 1 Cor. 1:10–13; 2 Cor. 11:4; Gal. 1:9; 2 Thess. 3:6, 14; 1 Tim. 1:3; 6:3.

[314] 1 John 2:18–19; 4:3; 2 John 7–11.

chosen by God to become His adopted children, God does not abandon the rest of humanity.

St. Jerome (345–420), a Doctor of the Church, affirmed that "ignorance of the Scripture is ignorance of Christ."[315] Sacred Scripture is the Word of God communicated in human language. St. Bonaventure (1221–1274), another Doctor of the Church, rightly insisted that "the source of Sacred Scripture was not human research but divine revelation."[316] God's divine message is transmitted by using a means that humanity understands. Since we are unable to speak the language of God, He speaks our language. It is similar to a family in which the parents speak to their child. They do not use complex "grown-up" language because the child is unable to understand what is being said. Rather, they go down to the level of the child and use words and gestures that the child can understand at whatever level of intellectual development he or she has attained. God does something similar with all of us.

Pope Francis enunciated it so aptly: "Sacred Scripture is a *Story of stories*."[317] Sacred Scripture cannot remain just printed words, for its reader is invited to pray about, meditate on, and embody by putting into action the divine teachings found in the divine message.

The worrisome situation in which the world finds itself in these days presents us with similar challenges and reactions that faced the pious Jew of almost three thousand years ago. Fervent prayers are said by those who trust in God's power. Rosary beads are run through our fingers as Catholic sons and daughters of the Virgin Mother. Heads are prayerfully bowed in silent fear and anxiety by

---

[315] St. Jerome, *Commentary on the Book of Isaiah*, prologue.

[316] St. Bonaventure, *Breviloquium*, 5, p. 201.

[317] Pope Francis, Message for the 54th World Communications Day (January 24, 2020), no. 3.

people of all faiths. We plead with God, like the pious Jew of many centuries ago, to protect us and our loved ones and to banish from earth our enemies. We ask the Lord to come to our assistance and to deliver us from the present evil.

The Jews of the Old Testament experienced plagues, famines, great social unrest and upheaval, national chaos, opportunist thugs, bogus prophets who agitated and misled them, family crises, grave economic calamities, fear of vandalism, restriction of movement due to fear of many forms of personal harm, great worries about their own family and loved ones, serious diseases—the list goes on. Like the pious Jew, let us place on our lips those words that came from the depths of their hearts: "Let thy steadfast love, O LORD, be upon us, even as we hope in thee,"[318] and, "When I am afraid, I put my trust in thee. In God, whose word I praise, in God I trust without a fear."[319]

Catholics and Old Testament Covenants

After the Habiru tribes (the Jews) made a successful departure from the land of Goshen in Egypt, they were no longer slaves. They were finally free from the yoke of Pharaoh. But they were far from free of the intricacies of dealing among themselves, for they were a very bellicose group of people. They could not appreciate, much less handle, their freedom. They did not have a stillness in their world, which was full of chaos. They were like those nations who used to be under the complete dominance of the Soviet Union. People who resisted this domination had a common enemy: the USSR. Once that yoke became a thing of the past, their national unity disappeared, as there was and remains

[318] Ps. 33:22.
[319] Ps. 56:3-4.

much upheaval in many of the newly established free countries. A similar story is also found in the former European colonies on the continent of Africa. Even our great country is presently at odds with itself, as people are abusing their freedom and perceive those who resist or do not adhere to their ideologies and/or their political party as some kind of an enemy. We are not handling our freedoms—which were won for us by our ancestors—in a positive and constructive manner.

God spoke to Moses through the burning bush[320] and gave him a twofold mission. One was to go and tell Pharaoh to "let my people go." The second was to lead them to the Promised Land. Both proved to be a test for Moses' faith. Both involved the desert: God spoke to Moses in the desert before the Exodus event and afterwards during the wanderings of the Hebrews in the Sinai Desert. In other words, God met Moses in the desert.

Let us pause for a moment and look at Moses: he was raised as an Egyptian prince. Though not an Egyptian, his adoptive mother made sure he was treated as any Egyptian prince might expect to be. He was well known in the palace and lived a very privileged lifestyle. He also certainly knew the Pharoah with whom he would eventually clash. They played together as children, and they grew up into young men.

Moses was also well acquainted with the Egyptian gods and rituals. No one knows if he joined in worshipping the endless number of Egyptian gods. But there is one hint that points to Moses being exposed to the God of his Hebrew ancestors: his mother and sister practically raised him until he returned to the palace to his adopted mother—the sister of the old Pharaoh.[321] Was Moses

---

[320] Exod. 3:1–4:17.
[321] Exod. 2:1–10.

conflicted in his religious beliefs? Did he only worship the God of his mother and sister, or did he also worship the Egyptian idols?

Now, let us look at our own lives. Most of us probably came from educated families. We received some sacraments as young children and in our youth. We were taught about God. We were taken to church to worship God, especially on Sundays. Were we conflicted like Moses when we went through some rebellious stage in our lives—when we rebelled against our parents, or perhaps against their Catholic Faith? Were we rebellious because we were told over and over again: "Do not," or, "It is wrong," or, "It is a sin," or, "Get out of bed and go to Mass"? Were we conflicted like Moses to be instructed about God, but then we also wanted to worship our idols like popularity, sports, wealth, or sex?

Moses tried to help the underdog: he went to the rescue of a Jew who was being abused by an Egyptian—but then he took the law into his own hands and murdered the slave driver.[322] Perhaps there were times when we rose to defend an underdog, someone who was the receiver of people's unkindness or demeaning and bullying behavior.

Moses had to flee, and he fled to the desert.[323] There, he met God in the form of a burning bush. God did not only give Moses a very challenging mission—to lead the Hebrew slaves out of Goshen and out of Egypt—but God also revealed His name to Moses: YAHWEH, meaning *I Am Who Am.*[324] God is not restricted by the laws of nature, and so, the bush burned but was not consumed by fire.[325] The true God, unlike the Egyptian gods,

---

[322] Exod. 2:11–12.
[323] Exod. 2:15.
[324] Exod. 3:14.
[325] Exod. 3:2.

has no beginning, is not the work of human hands or ingenuity, is not restricted to one place. God is pure spirit, and He is not bound to space. Thus, God cannot be held in a person's hands and moved from one place to another, unlike the Egyptian idols. The Egyptians prayed to a god that was located in a specific place or area, and then would pray to another god in another area or, at times, take their gods with them. However, Yahweh, since He is not limited by space, can be prayed to in any place. One can speak to the real God anywhere.

Recently, we experienced being limited due to the desert of lockdown and other restrictions. Did we meet God? Did God speak to us about our slavery to worldliness? Did He show us our limitations, our sinfulness, our reliance on things and values that make no difference in the long run? Did we learn the real value of our freedom? Have we learned anything of how precious and fragile life is and that we should focus our attention on the precious value of life, yours and mine and others'? Have we learned how to pray better and to rely more on God and His love, forgiveness of our sins, and mercy?

God told Moses very clearly that the descendants of Abraham were His people. He was there to protect them, to rescue them, to set them free so that He would meet them in the Sinai Desert. God had taken this enslaved and divided race and transformed them into His very own people. We, too, as Christians by virtue of our Baptism, have been taken by God to become members of His people.

So, let us join the inspired Psalmist and say, "Through thy precepts I gain understanding; therefore I hate every false way. Thy word is a lamp to my feet and a light to my path. I have sworn an oath and confirmed it, to observe thy righteous ordinances. I am sorely afflicted, give me life, O LORD, according to thy word! Accept my offerings of praise, O LORD, and teach me thy ordinances."[326] It is God who leads us through the desert of life and so, let us hear God say again, "I am continually with thee; thou dost hold my right hand."[327]

It has been stated the the implications of Moses meeting God in the desert and God giving Moses two missions, to tell Pharaoh to let God's people go and to lead the Hebrews to the Promised Land, proved to be very taxing on Moses. I am sure he spent many a sleepless night.

God won in the end! An obstinate and autocratic Pharaoh was finally compelled to let the Hebrew slaves leave Egypt. The tenth plague, the death of the firstborn sons, proved to be too much for Pharaoh and his countrymen. The Egyptians were very happy to see them go and showered them with precious gifts, including gold. Imagine being a slave one day and the next being given not only your freedom but a great fortune! This is what happened the day after the tenth plague visited Egypt. The loss of life experienced on a very personal level forced Pharaoh to free his Hebrew slaves.[328] We might ask ourselves: What would be required of me to let go of my slavery to worldly values and the world's ways of doing things—and to better appreciate other people? Do I need some catastrophe to wake me up to the reality that I am a sinner in dire need of God's boundless mercy?

Moses led the Hebrew former slaves into the desert of Sinai. The first challenge was to distance himself and his people from the Egyptians. He had to overcome the barrier of water, namely the waters of the Red Sea. So God empowered Moses to part the

---

[326] Ps. 119:104-108.
[327] Ps. 73:23.
[328] Exod. 12.

waters, to lead the people on dry land across to the other side, and then to allow the waters to come back together and engulf their enemy. Unfortunately, the freed Hebrew slaves did not appreciate what God had already done for them. They grumbled and complained. They looked back at their former place of slavery and said, "Those were good times!" We might say that they were a bunch of losers. Let us not rush to judgment, for our behavior might be putting us in the same boat!

Like Pharoah, we may be reluctant to let go of our power over others. Like the Hebrews, we may even be reluctant to let go of our slavery! Like Pharaoh, we might think that we are better than God in the choices we make. Like the Hebrews, we might long for the good old days of our slavery to ambition and passions because we might feel tired traveling toward the Promised Land—that is, Heaven.

The pious Jew, seeing all the headaches that his people gave to Moses and their infidelity to God, frequently asked the question: Why did You choose us, an insignificant and troublesome people? Yet Moses said, "For you are a people holy to the LORD your God; the LORD your God has chosen you to be a people for his own possession, out of all the peoples that are on the face of the earth. It was not because you were more in number than any other people that the LORD set his love upon you and chose you, for you were the fewest of all peoples; but it is because the LORD loves you, and is keeping the oath which he swore to your fathers."[329]

God personally chose you and me to be members of His new people, participants in His New Covenant, not because of our intelligence, good looks, talents, wealth, or education, but because He loves us.

[329] Deut. 7:6–8.

Moses continued to lead the complaining Hebrews across the desert. He led them to Mount Sinai. It is here that Moses encountered God again and He spoke once more to Moses. God made another covenant as a follow-up to His covenant with Abraham. This second covenant provided the Jews with a new lifestyle: the Ten Commandments. Many times we look at these Commandments as a list mainly of prohibitions. But, in fact, they are more than this. They speak about commitment and the living out of that commitment to God and in our interpersonal dealings. Thus, they state that allegiance must be to the One True God, for He is all-holy. One day of the week must be dedicated to God, and every day of the week should be lived in God's time and not ours. We are bound to honor and respect our parents and other people at all times, safeguarding every life, to live in the integrity of our marriage bond, always tell the truth, and rejoice in other people's success.

While God was speaking with Moses, the ever-dissatisfied former slaves looked back at the years in Goshen and longed for them, despite their former very oppressive slavery and the murder of their newborn sons. So, they abandoned God and began worshipping an idol—the golden calf, made of golden Egyptian gifts. One might say that they went mad and forgot how much God, their saving God, had done for them. This act of abandoning God began a pattern that was repeated throughout the Old Testament and that Christians have duplicated since the beginning of the Church.

Following a cycle of infidelity, the Jews told the prophet Samuel that they wanted to be like their neighbors: they wanted a king.[330] In a way, one might say that they wanted to conform to secular society. Up until then, it was God who was deemed the sole Ruler of Israel through His chosen agents, such as the judges. Samuel

---

[330] 1 Sam. 8:1–20.

was not pleased, for the people's demand was a direct affront to God. But God told Samuel to give them a king. The king was to become God's representative to His people.

Alas, the first king, Saul, was a complete disaster in the end—and no different from the people he ruled. He was at times faithful to God and at other times so in love with his power that he became unfaithful to God. Finally, God rejected Saul and ordered Samuel to seek out a new king. This newcomer's name was David,[331] and he was only a shepherd boy when the prophet chose him out. We are all familiar with David. However, many forget that David, the Lord's anointed, was not always faithful to God. He was adulterous, a murderer, a very proud man. Yet he always ended up regretting his sins and truly repenting of them. God loved him and made a covenant with him, promising that his royal house would never be extinguished.[332]

Regrettably, it did not take long for David's descendants to become notorious idolaters after the Kingdom of David was divided into two mini-kingdoms of Israel and Judah.[333] Granted, there were a handful of kings who were faithful to God and authentic reformers, but they were a minority. God sent His prophets to denounce idolatry, injustice, oppression of the weak and the poor and widows and orphans, and treaties that purported to show that the king no longer relied on the power of God but on his own powers, wealth, and success. The prophets were usually ignored, scoffed at, or persecuted. God respected the right of the kings and their subjects to opt for evil and sinful ways. But the many infidelities of the kings and their subjects led to doom. So, the Kingdom of Israel disappeared. The royal family of Judah and the

---

[331] 1 Sam. 15:1–35; 16:12–13.

[332] 2 Sam. 7:16.

[333] 1 Kings 12:1–17.

majority of Jews were exiled to Babylon. The walls of the Holy City of Jerusalem were destroyed. The Temple of Jerusalem, wherein dwelt God's glory, was desecrated and then razed to the ground.

Yet, throughout all of these centuries and horrible events, there was always a small group of people who remained faithful to God. They also lived as exiles in Babylon and frequently recalled God's promises. They were called the *anawim*, the faithful remnant. They had stillness in their hearts because they relied on the Lord.

God sent them prophets to console them, to encourage them, and to give them hope. They were reminded that God is a loving God, a forgiving God, a merciful God, a faithful God who would bring them back to their original homeland. There are many beautiful passages that relate the messages of the prophets during the Babylonian Exile. It seems that there is one covenant that stands out because it points to another major covenant that God was about to make with the remnant of the faithful Jews living in exile. The prophet Jeremiah declared, "This is the covenant which I will make with the house of Israel after those days, says the LORD. I will put my law within them, and I will write it upon their hearts; and I will be their God, and they shall be my people."[334]

This covenant marks a major switch. It speaks of God reigning in one's heart. We, Christians, are the inheritors of these covenants: Abraham is our father in faith; we are heirs of the covenant God made with David, for we are anointed kings at Baptism and belong to a kingly people; and we also are the spiritual descendants of the *anawim*, for God's laws do not rule a territorial nation but the kingdom of hearts. God has made His ultimate covenant through Jesus Christ, and the covenants of the Old Testament are

[334] Jer. 31:33.

absorbed in it. God made this covenant with the family of baptized Christians—and we are members of that family.

In the end, the above covenants of the Old Testament, but especially the covenant of Jesus Christ, offer hope to all of us. Are we great sinners? Have we abandoned God and married the world? Have we claimed that our success and prosperity are due to our human ingenuity? Have we replaced God with the idols of worldly values and, therefore, lied when we claimed to be Christians? Have we abandoned God because we wanted to hold on to our sinful and unchristian ways? God says to you and me, "Do not become discouraged. Do not let the devil discourage you, for there is hope for you."

Our God is a merciful God, a forgiving God, a faithful God, a loving God. Jesus seeks us out, and like the shepherd did to the sheep that was lost and then found, He will carry us upon His shoulders. Like the Good Samaritan, He will look after our spiritual and relational wounds and our sins, and bring us healing. Like the father welcoming his prodigal son—a person who was irresponsible, very selfish, enamored with his passions and impulses, materialism, and so on—God will welcome us back and put on a great feast on our return to Him, for we were "lost and now are found," and "I tell you, there will be more joy in heaven over one sinner who repents than over ninety-nine righteous persons who need no repentance."[335] Therefore, God says to each of us, "Fear not, for I am with you; be not dismayed, for I am your God; I will strengthen you, I will help you, I will uphold you with my victorious right hand."[336] He will provide us with stillness in our hearts amidst all the chaos that surrounds us.

[335] Luke 15:7.
[336] Isa. 41:10.

Catholics and the Prophets

Many people seem to be mesmerized by prophecy. They want to know the future, in particular their own futures. But is that what we *really* want? Such a gift could easily turn out to be a curse, when someone tells us that at the age of forty we will lose our spouse, and at the age of fifty our grandchild will die of an overdose or in an accident or violently, and at the age of sixty our family will abandon us because we are very sick and have become a burden. Do we want all of this foreknowledge, while knowing full well that we cannot change anything?

For the most part, people who want to know their futures want to hear that their marriages and families will be great, that they and their spouses will grow old happily together, that they will be adored by their grandchildren, they will enjoy their health for a very long time, and that they will want for nothing throughout their lives.

But prophecy is much more than mere fortune-telling! The Old Testament prophets spoke about the past, the present, and sometimes the future. But in regards to the future, they spoke about two things. First was the short-term consequences the Israelites would face if they continued to disobey God. The second was more long-term. It was God's promise of a Savior.

The classical Old Testament prophets, living between the tenth and the sixth centuries BC, were manifestly aware of their vocations and realized that there was something special about themselves. They knew that their call was unique because they experienced God calling them personally and intimately, setting them apart from the rest of the people. They received their calling during a mystical experience that was initiated by God, wherein God communicated the divine mind and will and, in turn, God commissioned the prophet to be His mouthpiece to his fellow Jews.

However, each prophet had a distinct personal experience. Though set apart for the divine mission, he remained very much part of his people. Yet, he also knew that the divine message entrusted to him would usually go unheeded and might even evoke a very abusive response from its audience.

Catholics are anointed prophets at the time of Baptism. Thus, we are today's anointed prophets. Our call is to be like Jesus Christ, to bring Him to others, not only by speaking but also acting like Jesus and sharing His divine message. Granted, the greatest majority of us do not have a mystical experience wherein we hear God calling us and speaking to us directly. However, I am sure that some of those who became Catholic converts as adults might tell us that they felt God calling them to join our Church. It might not have been an overwhelming mystical experience, but nonetheless they felt the call on an intimate, personal level.

Who knows? Someone might have heard such a call through you! Perhaps you made them interested in the Catholic Church by the way you live and witness to the Faith. This is a concrete aspect of being a prophet.

Many of us might not be aware that being Catholic is a vocation, a calling uttered by God. He chose us and created the events that would bring this about. It is called divine providence. The fact is that no human being is an afterthought of God. Numberless people are not aware of this fact. Others, who know they have been anointed at their Baptism, find it difficult to accept the fact that they personally have been chosen by God. They feel so insignificant! But the fact remains: we are God's chosen ones, for we belong to the household of God, with Jesus for a brother. We are called *Christians* because we, without any personal merit, belong to Christ.[337]

---

[337] Acts 11:26.

Like the prophets of the Old Testament, were called and set apart. Our mission is to bring the world the message of the God-made-Man, the promises of redemption and salvation. It is the mandate Jesus gave to His followers right before He ascended back into Heaven.[338] Like those ancient prophets, we live in the world, but do not belong to the world. We speak the language of our people and should use that language to speak God's message of love, salvation, mercy, forgiveness, and compassion. Like the ancient prophets, we know that in today's world the divine message and its messenger will not be well received. We have to just look at the moral mess our country is in because our laws are no longer based on revealed truth and natural law.

When the Old Testament prophets accepted their calling — though some did so with great difficulty, such as Jonah and Jeremiah — they lived in intimate terms with God. They received courage to proclaim the divine message. They became extremely sensitive to good and evil, instinctively knew what is right and wrong, and identified what was moral and immoral.

Now, when it comes to us as today's prophets: Have we accepted our calling to bring Jesus to others? How well do we carry out this divine vocation?

God has given us all the courage we need to fulfill our vocation as His prophets. We received this courage as one of the seven gifts of the Holy Spirit bestowed on those who are confirmed. We must change our lives. We must learn to be kind to those who are always in a bad mood. We must be supportive of those who have hurt us deeply. We must forgive those who attack our reputation with lies and gossip. We must clearly state what is right and what is wrong, regardless of what others may think of us. We must calmly

[338] Luke 24:50-51; Acts 1:9-11.

and respectfully, yet clearly and boldly, denounce what is evil in society. We must uphold what is moral rather than going along with a mob mentality. The ancient prophets were not strangers to all of the above. They paid a price for their witness. Are we willing to do the same? Will we accept the cost of living as Catholics and bringing God to others? The prospect is frightening, but God will give the grace of courage to those who ask for it.

The monarchy (which lasted for a little over four hundred years, ending with the Babylonian Exile) was the most difficult age for the prophets. Israel wanted to have a king like the surrounding pagan nations; as we said, God obliged and directed a very unhappy Samuel to anoint Saul as the nation's first king.[339] The king was to be God's anointed and favored one. God went ever so far as to establish a covenant with King David, promising that his kingdom would not pass away.[340] But this status did not stop most of David's successors from being evil, idolatrous, proud, adulterous, unjust, murderous, greedy, and oppressive. So God raised great prophets to take to task such kings and their powerful, corrupt agents.

The prophet's role was to reestablish the central place of the covenant of Sinai in Hebrew society, while his king was doing his best to supplant and replace it.

Many prophets recalled God's love and mercy toward the ancestors of their audience. Prophets recalled what had happened when their ancestors betrayed the allegiance to their compassionate and forgiving God. There followed national disasters and unbearable hardships. There had been foreign powers dominating, oppressing,

---

[339] 1 Sam. 8:6, 19, 22.
[340] 2 Sam. 7:16; 1 Kings 9:5.

and enslaving their forbears. Next, when the errant and repentant people turned back to God, He forgave them and came to their rescue. Then the king and his agents would go back to the offensive and sinful lifestyle that had brought so much suffering on their ancestors. So, it was only a matter of time until a great backlash came. Eventually, some prophets spoke about the future: if king and subjects did not repent and change their ways, the two kingdoms (Israel and Judah) would come to an end, their enemies would conquer and destroy all that was of value to the Jews, and they would carry them off into exile.

Eventually, the Jews *were* exiled. Yet, even then, God sent prophets to those living in exile and promised those who were faithful to Him, the remnant of Israel, that He would bring them back to their motherland, would restore the kingdom as a kingdom of faithful hearts, and would again descend in His glory into the reconstructed Temple of Jerusalem, for He would dwell again among His chosen ones. The people were asked to hope, to be faithful to God, to be patient, and to persevere. God would always fulfill His promises to them.

Now more than ever, our role as anointed prophets is similar to that of the classical prophets of the Old Testament. The United States has bragged for a number of centuries that it is a Christian nation, that it abides with Christian principles. But, if we look around us, we know that this is not true. We simply have to look at the way many people are being treated because of the color of their skin, their national origins, their religious beliefs, their gender, their physical appearance and mental capacity, their accent, and so forth. Our laws have redefined moral norms and equated feeling good with being good. They have deified personal interests and personal rights at the cost of the common good. We have even gone so far as to reject our natural gender and assume a different designation. We have redefined the marriage covenant. We have established a system to prioritize who should live and who should die.

In other words, we have become irresponsible and disinterested in the laws of nature. Such a mentality is similar to those evil kings confronted and denounced by the prophets for their wickedness. We have exiled ourselves from the true God. As prophets, our mission is to restore God's prominence in our personal lives, to work for the restoration of the Christian message as not being only in terms of freedom of worship and right to assemble, but as a living code of life. This mission is not a solitary one, for we belong to the Church, to the family of God. Like the faithful Jews living during the Babylonian Exile, we are asked to hope, to be faithful to God, to be patient, to be still in our hearts, and to persevere, for God assuredly will fulfill His promises.

Let us hear those beautiful words that God directed the prophet Jeremiah to proclaim, though the prophet complained of the way he was treated by his fellow countrymen: "Now the word of the LORD came to me saying, before I formed you in the womb I knew you, and before you were born I consecrated you; I appointed you a prophet to the nations."[341] Let us also hear what God told the prophet Isaiah to tell His people: "Fear not, for I have redeemed you; I have called you by name, you are mine"[342]; and what the Lord Himself assures those who are faithful to Him: "Rejoice that your names are written in heaven."[343] There is much reason to find our stillness in God amidst the upheaval that is surrounding us.

[341] Jer. 1:5.
[342] Isa. 43:1.
[343] Luke 10:20.

Then and Now: The Cycle Repeats Itself

So, with all that has been stated in this section with reference to our Old Testament heritage, where do we stand? Authentic Catholics do not sit on a fence and play it safe. The second great commandment, love your neighbor as yourself,[344] denies us the chance to be passive prophets.

One of the major deficiencies in the United States' general population is a pronounced lack of appreciation for history. There abounds in our midst that great feature of cancel culture, thereby making it more complicated. Instead of enriching and expanding our knowledge, we are robbed of our national memory.

The recent toppling or relocating of statues is a good example. For better or for worse, those people formed part of our nation's history. Whether we like it or not, these people form part of our nation's history and national family. Just as we cannot completely disown our ancestors, for we remain inheritors of their DNA, so, too, we cannot disown such people from our nation's history. Perhaps we should erect monuments beside them of those they oppressed to provide us with a broader and more informed picture of our nation's history.

Who knows? Next, there might even be demands to change names of cities founded by Catholic missionaries who dedicated them to some divine mystery (such as Sacramento) or a saint (such as San Antonio).

Many people spend lots of money and energy to travel to Italy or Greece or Egypt to marvel at the ancient world and its works of art. Billions of dollars have been spent over the years to restore and preserve such objects. Many kinds of businesses are established to accommodate tourists. Visitors pay to see statues and palaces like

---

[344] Matt. 7:12; 22:39; Mark 12:31; Luke 6:31.

those of the Emperors Nero, Marcus Aurelius, Diocletian, Trajan, Hadrian, and Valerian, or to view an artwork by Caravaggio, or a book by Machiavelli, or some rare ancient Greek vase, or the great pyramids.

Little do they know that those ancient Roman emperors were not only dictators, but murdered their opponents. Some had their family members executed. Others enslaved entire nations. Many of them martyred Christians and destroyed early churches. At one point, 90 percent of the population in Rome was made up of slaves who kept Rome functioning.

Perhaps these tourists do not know that the genius Caravaggio was a murderer and substance abuser. I am sure they know that when there is some sinister or evil motive, it is called Machiavellian. But do they realize that Greece was famous not only for its philosophers and culture, but also for the sexual abuse of minors and cultural genocide?

Perhaps these visitors have not been told that the builders of the pyramids were slaves and that the Pharaohs practiced incestuous marriages between father and daughter and brother and sister—many times when the girl was not yet a teen. As for the Incas, the Mayans, and the Aztecs, three great ancient civilizations in our hemisphere, they practiced human sacrifice, with frequent child sacrifices.

Is it not ironic that modern barbarians, busy destroying recent history, approach these ancient monuments and artifacts of ancient civilizations in a different way? Some of them would no doubt go so far as to condemn people who destroyed such ancient sites! If we are to follow the reasoning of modern iconoclasts, then we should deface or topple or dismantle or destroy anything that reminds us of the dark side of the ancient and recent past. Perhaps in this instance such destructive agitators might come to realize the importance of protecting history, including all of its wrinkles.

It is stated that history is always written by the conqueror. By the same token, the voice of the conquered falls silent. Yet, no matter what we *remember* (or forget!), nothing can change what *happened.*

The ancient Jews lived through great and deplorable times. They were firsthand witnesses of great achievements and terrible destruction. It is never forgotten that most of today's Jews are the descendants of the Hebrew slaves who lived in Goshen. The Jews of ancient times looked at their history not as a simple, faithful report and recollection of a series of events. Rather, they viewed it as a series of events that evoked the basic question: Where is God in all of these events? They tried to find God in history. And God sent not only heroes but villains.

The Jews knew that there was a reason for all of this. God permitted evil to happen, though evil was not God's doing but man's. Thus, their recounting of history is not a scientific reporting of events, but a theological interpretation and understanding of events. It was written and read by the light of faith. Theirs was a history of how God dealt with humanity, and particularly with His Chosen People, Israel. We and the ancient Jews are reminded of what God proclaimed through the prophet Isaiah: "For my thoughts are not your thoughts, neither are your ways my ways."[345]

I referred above to a definitive pattern of how sacred history is presented in the Old Testament, and perhaps we and our contemporary society might learn something from it. It always involved five phases.

First, the Jewish people, as a unit and as individuals, was reminded of God's special love. Out of love God created them, and out of love God chose them to be His people.

---

[345] Isa. 55:8.

Second, they were reminded of their sins as a nation and as individuals. It was the people and not God who sinned. They were the ones, collectively and individually, who chose to violate the divine covenant between God and His people.

Third, the nation and the individual were punished as a consequence of their transgressions.

Fourth is the realization that their calamity was incurred through their disobedience to God. The Jews cried out to God, asking to be forgiven and delivered. They expressed true contrition. They vowed to dedicate themselves to God and not to put their trust in idols or human powers.

Fifth, a faithful and loving God, a forgiving and merciful God, a redeeming and saving God, heard the contrite cry of His people. He forgave them and came to their rescue.

Unfortunately, this cycle was to repeat itself frequently.

Is this not also our personal story? Is not this cycle in the Jewish sacred history the same cycle that takes place in our personal lives and in our communities?

First, we are not created as the result of some accident. A human being might claim that a baby's conception was "an accident," but this is not true. Chance has no part in divine providence. No human being is conceived unless God not only allows it but participates in the creation of human life. The biological parents might perceive the conception as a "mistake," but God never makes such mistakes. Furthermore, one of the reasons why artificial birth control is immoral is that the couple chooses to limit artificially God's creative powers by using drugs or through man-made devices.

Second, we are reminded that we form part of a fallen nature due to Original Sin. All of us are sinners. There are only two persons who are not touched by sin: Jesus and His Mother Mary. No one else is exempt. We are sinners. Those who claim that they are not sinners are lying to themselves and living in a world of denial and sheer fantasy. They are in very serious trouble because they put themselves outside God's loving redemption.

We, as individuals, may be guilty of a variety of sins, big and small. But, as was the case with the ancient Jews of the Old Testament, we also sin as a nation. We must be mindful that we are the ones who sin individually and collectively and choose to violate the divine covenant. There are plenty of sins as a nation: racism, police brutality, corruption, the sale of pornography, euthanasia, the abandonment of the elderly, environmental destruction, unjust wages, the lack of moral courage in some religious and many civil leaders, no-fault divorce, and of course, abortion. All of these are found in the United States. We as a nation lack a sense of sin.

So, we go our way as individuals and as a community and fantasize that all is well as long as it does not touch me or my family. But we have to be reminded of sin, not in a scrupulous way—for that is most unhealthy and psychologically problematic—but by a gentle invitation to have an honest look at our personal lives and lives as a nation. In a way, this involves a personal as well as a national examination of conscience.

Third, like the Jews of the Old Testament, we are punished both as individuals and as a community for our sins. In these instances, we tend to perceive God not as pure spirit, thus devoid of moods and passions, but in terms of being "human." We try to blame our suffering on God's anger, as if God has a nasty temper! Rather, God accepts our free choices and tolerates our sinful decisions and acts. Yet He also provides us with every grace to help us make the right choices, but He will never help us make bad decisions. He never abandons us!

Fourth, Jesus, the Good Shepherd, always seeks out the lost sheep. Our loving God does not give up on the sinner but sends all the graces necessary for conversion, for a turning-back to Him.

God never gives up on us! He provides us with the grace and strength to look at where we are and realize that we need divine assistance. We turn back to God, perhaps out of great disillusionment or frustration or even shame, and cry out for deliverance from our misery. We express true contrition because we realize that we have sinned, that we are leading sinful lifestyles. We recognize our mistakes. We come to comprehend that we have bought into a set of values that are self-absorbed, self-righteous, destructive, unloving, hateful, and unchristian. We have gravely sinned and, with true contrition, we turn back to God, acknowledge our sinfulness, and promise to amend our lives and cry out to Him: *Save me! Save our community!* We join the Psalmist in crying out: "Out of the depths I cry to thee, O LORD! Lord, hear my voice! Let thy ears be attentive to the voice of my supplications!"[346] Let us hear God speaking to us through the prophet Isaiah, saying, "Every one who thirsts, come to the waters,"[347] and through the prophet Jeremiah, saying, "I will satisfy the weary soul, and every languishing soul I will replenish."[348]

Let us listen to the Lord saying to us, "Come to me, all who labor and are heavy laden, and I will give you rest. Take my yoke upon you, and learn from me; for I am gentle and lowly in heart, and you will find rest for your souls."[349] We should never be discouraged to approach the Lord.

[346] Ps. 130:1–2.
[347] Isa. 55:1.
[348] Jer. 31:25.
[349] Matt. 11:28–29.

Fifth, and last in the cycle, is the fact that a faithful and loving God, a forgiving and merciful God, a redeeming and saving God, hears our contrite cry. He forgives us. As Pope Francis stated on June 29, 2020: "Even though we often go to God only in moments of need, God sees beyond and invites us to go further, to seek not only His gifts, but Him; to entrust to Him not only problems, but life."[350] The Lord provides us with the Sacrament of Reconciliation and absolves our sins, and we are back in His company because He is our God and we are His people. We seek tranquility in our world full of turmoil. We achieve this when we have stillness in the Lord.

---

[350] Pope Francis, Angelus for the Feast of Saints Peter and Paul (June 29, 2020).

7

The Silence of God

God's Silence—and Ours

There is an old saying: all roads lead to Rome. However, we should be saying that all good roads lead to Heaven! This thoroughfare involves the presence of silence on God's side, as well as our silence. This silence is not that we simply say nothing, as if we were statues, but that we listen attentively and prayerfully. It is a type of silence that involves our lips, our hearts, our emotions, and our brains.

There might be many moments or even years when we feel that God seems to be deaf, and therefore silent, to our worries. How should we react to this silence of God? How can this silence change our way of looking at our faith and our prayer lives? How can these changes affect our journey toward Heaven? After all, life is a pilgrimage—one that should end with our entrance into God's eternal dwelling place. God created us out of love just for this purpose: to live in His heavenly home, where there is no measurement of time.

When Pope Francis visited Naples in 2015, one of his events involved meeting with the youth, the future of our Church. During that meeting, the pope said, "Our God is a God of words, gestures and silences!"[351] Then, he made reference to the Parable of the Good Shepherd.[352] We are all familiar with this parable. The pope said that God is a God who knows us better than we know ourselves, and who speaks to us in the silence of our hearts. Pope Francis went on to say that God cannot speak to us if we are not silent, if we do not silently gaze at the crucifix. He said that we can draw near to the silence of God by contemplating Christ Crucified and abandoned.

"Unless we are silent." This makes a lot of sense. I, by nature, tend to avoid noisy places and people. But I frequently fail. When people talk at the same time, be it at the dinner table, in a restaurant, during a heated argument, at a friendly gathering, or at any kind of get-together, it seems like everyone is talking and no one is listening because everyone is trying to get his or her point across.

I remember that when I was a young priest, I wanted to make a retreat at a Trappist monastery. Finally, one day, the opportunity arose. Trappists are expected to live their lives in silence, and when I arrived, I told the retreat master that I wished to follow the schedule of the monks. Since they begin the day at 2:00 a.m., he came to wake me up at 1:30 a.m. Once I got ready, I went to the sacristy. In huge letters, written on each of the sacristy walls, there was the word shouting at everyone: SILENTIUM. *Silence.* Well, I was not there yet a minute when the abbot came in and darted toward me to greet me and to welcome me as "the man from Rome," as if I was an authority of some kind. Then he began asking me how things were in Rome. He went on speaking about

---

[351] Pope Francis, Meeting with Youth in Naples (March 22, 2015).
[352] John 10:1–18.

the situation of the Church in Ireland and that we should be pray-ing very hard, for Ireland was heading toward a great crisis in the Catholic Faith—something that proved to be prophetic. Silence for me in the sacristy lasted about one minute, despite that huge word inscribed on the walls!

A friend, who had come on the retreat with me, decided to exercise his own version of silence by sleeping the entire night until Holy Mass. Maybe he chose the better portion!

Next, I lined up with the monks to process to the abbey's cha-pel, where the monks sang the Office of Readings, and sang it so beautifully. This was followed by thirty minutes of silent medita-tion. Then the monks lined up silently and exited from the chapel at 3:15 a.m. Everyone went back to his room to get some more sleep. At 6:00 a.m., there was the chanting of Morning Prayer and the celebration of Holy Mass. Breakfast followed and was eaten in absolute silence. I was getting pleased with this setup, despite the initial mishap.

After breakfast, the monks went to do whatever they were as-signed to do, mostly manual labor, and I decided to take a walk on the abbey grounds. Big mistake! I was walking silently for about fifteen minutes when this crowd of men invaded the abbey. They were there for a three-day retreat, and they belonged to one of Ireland's Alcoholics Anonymous groups. I think what attracted their attention was the fact that there was a priest, wearing black, and not wearing the habit of a Trappist monk. I stood out like a sore thumb, and they immediately knew I was an outsider.

Next thing I knew, three of them cornered me and—typical of the Irish friendly character—began asking me all kinds of ques-tions. Then they decided to share their individual stories, how AA was helping them, and that they were there on a silent retreat. Imagine, a silent retreat while they were chatting their heads off!

There went the silence and my silent retreat! Others in the group continued to seek me out after their meetings. So, after two more days, my friend and I decided to flee the abbey and cut short our so-called silent retreat!

Now to get back to the pope in Naples. Francis, in responding to a question about the silence of God, told the young people that God created us to be happy, but that this does not mean that everything in life is perfect simply because we believe in God. He said that one of the great silences of God regards the reason for suffering children. He said that we cannot always understand the silence of God, suggesting that we have to get closer to Christ on the Cross in silence. Perhaps, in moments that we see children suffering and dying, we should be mindful that God is taking note of all of these mind-blowing events and is busy preparing a place for the child at His side.

I recommend that we practice such silence, meaning moments in which we quietly place our confidence in God. We might try to be silent for fifteen minutes a day. It might be difficult at first, since our society exists in a cacophony that assaults our every waking hour. It is a disease, causing untold physical and mental and spiritual harm.

Of course, there is healthy silence and destructive silence. There is the destructive silence of spouses refusing to speak to one another, or of parents to their children or relatives, or of children to their parents and siblings, or to coworkers, and so forth. This kind of silence is a form of punishment. It is silence-as-injustice.

Then there is the silence in front of violence. We witness someone committing a crime, but we do nothing. This kind of silence is rooted in fear or indifference. There is the silence of not helping someone in need, and we walk away. The BBC news recently had a very eye-opening special report entitled, "Homeless in London: 'People Pretend They Are Not There.' "[353] It happens all over the world. This kind of silence is a violation of Christian love.

But there is also positive and productive silence. This silence is present between two people deeply in love and who are simply present to each other. This kind of silence could be the expression of such unsaid words as "I love just being with you, near to you. I don't, you don't, have to say anything." In a way, this kind of silence is almost divine, for it reminds us of the silent presence of God, who is deeply in love with us. There is the silence of being in God's presence and praying. We are waiting in silence for God to speak, in the attentive way we deal with human beings. In other words, there is the silence of the mouth and of the mind. We are not only physically quiet but also *silent*.

I visited Lebanon some time ago as a guest of the country's papal nuncio. One day he took me to see some places outside Beirut. One of the places was what the New Testament called the land of the Samaritans. We visited a village where, according to ancient tradition, Jesus encountered the Samaritan woman at Jacob's well.[354] There was a magnificent church being built at the time and the ceiling was already covered with brilliant mosaics. Some two hundred yards outside the church, there is a statue of a beautiful young woman, sitting and waiting. They call it "Our Lady of Awaiting." It is a stunning statue of Our Lady waiting for her Son. Ancient local tradition, both Christian and Muslim, has it that Our Lady waited there in silence for her Son to return from

---

[353] BBC, "Homeless in London: 'People Pretend They Are Not There,' " video by Rob Taylor, September 24, 2021, https://www.bbc.com/news/av/uk-england-london-58639151.

[354] John 4:4–42.

his trip to Tyre and Sidon. She was waiting immersed in prayer. This kind of silence is the nutrition for growing in holiness.

The Old Testament has many examples of the silence of God, beginning with the first chapter of the book of Genesis. The opening first two verses of the book of Genesis state, "In the beginning God created the heavens and the earth. The earth was without form and void, and darkness was upon the face of the deep; and the Spirit of God was moving over the face of the waters."[355] First, there was absolute silence on the part of God. Then God spoke and something began to happen: earth's Creation. The only time when God spoke in Creation was to create something out of nothing (for example, "Let there be light") and then to give a name to each of His creations: "God called the light Day, and the darkness he called Night."[356] God never spoke to any of His creatures—that is, except when it came to the first human couple, whom God created in His own image.[357] God allowed all created things to multiply and grow in silence. It continues to this very day: a silent seed is planted into silent soil, and the seed—in silence—germinates and begins to grow, and it overcomes the covering soil to sprout up and eventually to blossom into a plant or a flower or a fruit—all done in silence.

Not so with man and woman. God spoke to Adam and Eve. God did not remain silent. God specifically told the first couple to increase and multiply,[358] and God told them specifically not to eat of the tree of good and evil.[359] Jewish tradition has a very poetic way of describing the friendship between God and Adam

---

[355] Gen. 1:1–2.
[356] Gen. 1.5.
[357] Gen. 1:26–27.
[358] Gen. 1:28.
[359] Gen. 2:16–17.

and Eve. It states that God walked with them in the breeze, in the cool of the evening—and in silence. How romantic!

Yes, it is romantic, because God is deeply in love with humanity.

The silence of God was shuttered when Adam and Eve broke the law of God for the first time. It was only then that God spoke again. God had come for His usual walk with Adam and Eve in the cool of the evening.[360] They were not there! And God broke His silence: He asked Adam and Eve "Where are you?" God knew that they had sinned, but He wanted to find them and to take them back into His friendship. Adam responded by blaming Eve. Eve responded by blaming the serpent,[361] and mankind has been passing the buck ever since.

We lay blame for our sins on others, situations, pressure, mental duress, lack of sleep, lack of money, the undue pressures from Covid-19, and so forth. We have not been silent.

On the other hand, God wanted to walk again with Adam and Eve and their descendants in the cool of the evening, like two lovers holding hands and loving every second they are in each other's company without uttering a word. So, immediately God offered Adam and Eve hope: the promise of the Redeemer.[362] But, God was also compelled to act justly and to punish Adam and Eve for their transgression. So, God expelled our first parents from the Garden of Eden. Silence remained in the Garden until God's promises were fulfilled by sending His only-begotten Son into the world as our Savior and Redeemer—Jesus Christ.

Perhaps one of the longest silences of God that is easily overlooked is when He said nothing for a number of centuries after

---

[360] Gen. 3:8.
[361] Gen. 3:12–13.
[362] Gen. 3:15.

Jacob's extended family migrated to Goshen in the land of Egypt.[363] God was not absent, but He was silent, silently looking after the descendants of Abraham. And they were silent right back! I suspect that like us, when things go well, the protective silence of God is not really noticed. So, for a number of centuries, the protective silence of the God of Abraham, Isaac, and Jacob was not noticed by the Jews in Egypt because, thanks to Joseph, who had earned the trust of the Pharaoh,[364] they were well off. So, why mind God being silent?

Then, as the book of Exodus states, "There arose a new king over Egypt, who did not know Joseph."[365] That's when their troubles started. Eventually they were enslaved. The success story of an immigrant people was over. Indignity and abuse replaced joy and prosperity. So, they turned to God, and God sent them Moses.

At first, they liked him. Then, once they began the journey across the Sinai Desert to the Promised Land, they turned into constant complainers and idolaters. To state that they were a very unhappy bunch of people would be an understatement.

God led them, taught them, comforted them. But the hearts of the freed slaves were deaf. The noise of their complaints and anxieties drowned out the voice of God. Is not this also our story as a people and as individuals?

Listening to the Silence of God with Job

Sacred Scripture says that God knows us intimately, more deeply than we know ourselves, and He loves us. Knowing this should suffice. But does it?

---

[363] Gen. 46:28; 47:12.
[364] Gen. 41:37–40.
[365] Exod. 1:8.

Unfortunately, many people know God only through hearsay or solely on an intellectual level. But the more we are open to His silence, the more we begin to know Him truly. This supreme assurance, which opens the way to a profound encounter with God, matures in silence. St. Francis Xavier, exhibiting no self-interest, prayed, and said to the Lord, "I love You, not because You can give me heaven or condemn me to hell, but because You are my God. I love You, because You are You."

Job's experience as reported to us in Sacred Scripture is particularly significant in regard to God's silence. In one swift blow, the man lost everything: family, wealth, friends, and health.[366] It seemed that God's silence was one of absence. And yet, Job still spoke with God, cried out to God. Despite all that had happened to him, his faith was intact, though there were times when it was shaken to its core. In the end, he discovered the true value of his experience and of God's silence. Thus, eventually, turning to his Creator, he was able to conclude, "I had heard of thee by the hearing of the ear, but now my eye sees thee."[367] In other words, Job no longer relied on what others said about God, that is on hearsay, but on his firsthand experience of God.

Perhaps, Job is one of the greatest figures in the Old Testament for teaching us about listening to the silent God. We are all familiar with his story. But do we really understand it? Are we fully aware of the great questions about human life posed in the inspired book of Job? We usually look at Job as the ideal patient man. But in fact, it seems that while he listened to the silence of God with great patience, there was rising within him a great mute anger and anxiety. His soul was not still.

[366] Job 1:13–22.
[367] Job 42:5.

Job's suffering was emotional. He lost his family, his fortune, and his health. He eventually became a complaining man, plagued with suicidal thoughts, nightmares, and a sense of insignificance and self-hatred. He was haunted by the thought of God tormenting him. He despaired of his very life. As Job's spirit was being crushed, he showed indications of psychopathology: depression, hopelessness, loneliness, anxiety, fears, abandonment, and behavioral vacillations due to daydreaming.

Job's comforters only increased his suffering. They complicated matters. They blamed him for his misfortunes and invalidated his pain. They pointed out that he had the power to bring an end to his misery by simply acknowledging and repenting of his sin. They contended that his sufferings were self-induced, while Job repeatedly proclaimed his innocence. His friends could not accept his claim to innocence.

Job's suffering was also physical. He wept constant wept and slept little. His symptoms included festering wounds, blackened and peeling skin, and a fever. Job was in constant physical anguish.

Job's physical pain affected his emotional condition. When we are in pain, we are usually not very happy people. And although we know that his condition will not be fatal, Job had no assurance of this at the time. Rather, he was aware that although some skin diseases could heal, there were those that were terminal. However, Job also suffered at yet another level beyond the emotional and the physical.

Job's suffering was also spiritual. When Job first received word of the disasters that had befallen his family, his livestock, and his fortune, his response was acceptance and a renewed trust in God. I think many people of faith might initially respond in a similar way. Likewise, following the onset of his revolting skin disease that was added to his great losses, Job chose the same path. He resigned himself to the will of God.

Of course, an acceptance of continuous poverty and suffering might camouflage a resignation to evil and injustice. If we simply give up hope, we can never truly have faith. And this surely happened to Job. Job simply accepted the injustice of the situation. Like many of us might say, he said that his blamelessness did not deserve his pain. Now his faith was being challenged. Like many of us, he cried out: Why me? He no longer blindly accepted whatever he received from the hand of God. Job began to question God and His justice—and he questioned his faith. Does this have a familiar ring to it?

Job's most powerful encounter with God came by way of complaint, bewilderment, and confrontation. Job was thrown into a great conundrum, and eventually he began to question his God. "Why?" he cried out. Listen closely to God's answer: *nothing*. God answered with absolute silence. He did not speak, nor did He reveal His presence to Job.

Centuries later, St. John of the Cross (1542–1951) would describe this experience of silence as the "dark night of the soul."[368] Job called out to God. Job sought God. Yet God chose not to speak. Why?

One answer from the text is obvious: God's silence, and Job's faith in spite of that silence, were the point of the wager made between God and Satan. If only God had provided an inspiring pep talk: "Do this for Me, Job, and you will be a martyr and a man of great faith," and his situation might have become bearable. If God had spoken to Job, then Job, feeling the strength from the

---

[368] See St. John of the Cross, *Ascent of Mount Carmel* and *Dark Night of the Soul.*

voice of God, would have suffered gladly. I think if we hear God speaking to us and telling us that our suffering has a great purpose, and God explains it to us, then we would gladly suffer. However, Satan had claimed that Job's faith would not survive in the absence of such an explanation. When God accepted those terms, Job was robbed of spiritual sight and emotional comfort.

Faith, your faith and mine and Job's, demands that its object be hidden, or else it would not be faith. It would be sight. St. Paul stated that faith is the conviction of things not seen, but hidden,[369] silent. Therefore, in the case of Job (and in our own case as well), the point of the wager was to force a personal decision from Job: Would he continue in the way of faith even when that faith was unrewarded and painful? Or would he desert the God of his faith, as his wife suggested when she commented, "Do you still hold fast your integrity? Curse God, and die"?[370] In a way, one might say that Satan was posing this question. He used suffering as a weapon to strike down Job's faith—and he tries to do the same to us.

Faced with God's silence in the face of our suffering, we are presented with two basic options. First, we may choose to focus our attention not on ourselves, but on God. We may worship Him simply because He is our Lord, as pointed to above in the case of St. Francis Xavier. In this instance, we have faith, not with some expectation of reward, such as a cure from an illness, but because we trust in God. This is faith. The second is to place oneself at the center of existence. We know many a time that pain and suffering can lead to becoming more selfish, more self-centered, less kind, and very unchristian in our attitudes and behaviors.

---

[369] Heb. 11:1.
[370] Job 2:9.

Thus, God's silence in our sufferings brings us to a moment of decision. We must keep in mind that, as in the case of Job, listening to the silence of God in faith does not mean an end to suffering, but a purpose for it.

Job stopped listening to the silence of God and began to lament. He lamented (to the point of accusation) that God was hiding, abandoning him. Job, already emotionally abandoned by his so-called comforters, now knew what every sufferer realizes: suffering isolates the one who is suffering. Isolation adds the pain of loneliness and self-doubt. Much of Job's complaint centered around the isolation of his suffering. He felt the separation from God that resulted from his own preoccupation with his pain.

One major contributor to Job's emotional, mental, and spiritual anguish was God's apparent silence in the face of his great yet undeserved suffering. He began to question the God of his faith, to call upon God to explain what He was doing, to give an accounting of His actions, to break the silence. Why, he wondered, am I suffering when I am blameless? —something you and I might also ask ourselves at times. Why does God not intervene? Can we hear ourselves asking similar questions?

According to Job's friends, God acts according to justice.[371] Thus, they concluded that since Job was experiencing great suffering, he must have greatly sinned. After all, if Job were being punished for something he *hadn't* done, God could not be righteous and good.

On the other hand, according to Job, the wicked prosper, the weak are not protected, and good people suffer the same or worse fates as others.[372] In his first two responses, Job not only made his rebuttals

[371] Job 34:10.
[372] Job 21:7-17.

to his friends, but he also lodged his complaint to God. Additionally, in his final speech, Job laid out his argument. These "complaints" were more than simple words of bitterness. His "crying out" was not a mere cry for deliverance, but an appeal for justice. Job borrowed the language of litigation that he employed throughout his complaints to demand his vindication. Yet, in the end, he proclaimed, "I know that my Redeemer lives, and at last he will stand upon the earth."[373] Thus, he eventually realized and said that at some point he will be vindicated and declared innocent of any wrongdoing.

It is at this point that God chose to break His silence. God had remained silent when under sharp attack by an angry Job, but He now decided to set Job straight: suffering cannot be understood in every instance as a penalty for sin.

Here we have something that all of us should bear in mind: not all suffering is a punishment for sin. In no uncertain terms, God told Job that he has been operating under too rigid an understanding of who God is. God clearly made the point that life is much more complex than a simple formula. Human suffering is more than a system of rewards and punishments. The Lord is not of the hostage mentality of "Give to me, and I will give to you," of a *quid pro quo*. Thus, we should avoid such words as, "What have I done to deserve all of this suffering?"

When God finally spoke, after all that Job had experienced—loss, grief, depression, disease, ridicule, abandonment, and hopelessness—He provided Job with a perspective. God did not tell him everything. He never explained why Job had to suffer—why He never acted on Job's behalf, why He stayed silent for so long. On that topic, God's silence remained. Yet, at that moment, what God revealed to Job was enough.

[373] Job 19:25.

God gives us only partial answers, and we might walk away feeling very hurt due to His silence. He has spoken, but He has also not spoken. He has given us what He considers enough, but sometimes we crave more. That which we do not comprehend we label as a "mystery," even God's apparent silence. In the end, Job realized that joy is not the absence of pain but the presence of God.

Pope Francis points to the purpose of suffering: "Look at the crucifix in silence, look at the wounds, look at the heart of Jesus, look at the whole: Christ Crucified, the Son of God, annihilated, humiliated ... for love."[374]

The Silence of God in the Psalms

The silence of God is real. Many of us have experienced it personally. There are times when our hearts cry out to God, and there seems to be no response. We pray, pouring out our hearts, only to hear the words echo back without a reply. A crucial thing is that we have been conditioned to believe that there is a direct relationship between output and input, cause and effect. We expect an automatic interplay between what we do and what happens, as if our prayer lives are like being at a supermarket: we pay and we immediately receive the item we had paid for. When we cry out to God and nothing happens, how can we help but feel that something's not quite right—and that the problem is with the listener, with God, and not with us?

I think the best words of expressing this cry, this anguish, are found in the Psalms. Many of us mistake God's no or His "not yet" for silence. Perhaps one of the easiest ones that can be missed, though very important to attend to, is when we are experiencing "deep calling to deep."

---

[374] Pope Francis, Homily at Casa Santa Marta (April 22, 2020).

Let us consider the words of Psalm 42: "As a hart longs for flowing streams, so my soul longs for thee, O God. My soul thirsts for God, for the living God.... My tears have been my food day and night, while men say to me continually, 'Where is your God?'"[375] Here is someone who is hungering for a word from God. He or she alludes to a difficult time, a season of calling out to God in the midst of pain, grief, or confusion. From all angles, it appears as if God is silent to such cries—so much so that the bystanders might scoff, "Where is this God of yours that you pray to?" But notice what the Psalmist goes on to say: "Why are you cast down, O my soul, and why are you disquieted within me? Hope in God.... My soul is cast down within me; therefore I remember thee.... Deep calls to deep at the thunder of thy cataracts."[376]

The Psalmist comes to realize that there is no silence. Rather, there is an answer from God that is deeper than words and their sound. God is present and speaking, but what God is saying is not resting on the surface of the waters of life, but way underneath. This is a season where deep is calling to deep, so to speak. We should take into consideration that what we are encountering is not silence, but a pregnant pause; a prompting to engage in personal reflection so that the secret of answers, the most profound of responses, can be correctly heard and understood.

We go through seasons where God's answers do not come quickly or on the surface of things—when the way God interacts with our prayers draws us deeper into Him for guidance and trust, dependence, and obedience. These answers radically transcend what we initially sought to find. Thus, we might be introduced

[375] Ps. 42:1-3.
[376] Ps. 42:5-7.

to some sin we need to confront, to patterns of behavior we need to halt, to insights into who we are and what we did not have before, of the depths of a relationship with God that we had never experienced before. I believe that the Psalms seem to articulate our deepest feelings about the silence of God. Let us hear what the inspired Psalmists says about the silence of God in the midst of much personal suffering and darkness. I think we can identify with some of them.

There might be times when we feel victimized and powerless. Psalm 22 cries out, "My God, my God, why hast thou forsaken me? Why art thou so far from helping me, from the words of my groaning? O my God, I cry by day, but thou dost not answer."[377]

There might be times when people gossip about us and harm our integrity and reputation at work or in our community. Psalm 119 states, "With my whole heart I cry out; answer me, O LORD! I will keep thy statutes. I cry to thee; save me.... I rise before dawn and cry for help; I hope in thy words.... Hear my voice in thy steadfast love.... They draw near who persecute me with evil purpose; they are far from thy law.... Look at my affliction and deliver me, for I do not forget thy law. Plead my cause and redeem me; give me life according to thy promise!"[378]

There might be times when we are very discouraged by our sins. Psalm 130 cries out, "Out of the depths I cry to thee, O LORD! Lord, hear my voice! Let thy ears be attentive to the voice of my supplications! If thou, O LORD, shouldst mark iniquities, LORD, who could stand? But there is forgiveness with thee, that thou mayest be feared. I wait for the LORD, my soul waits, and in his word I hope; my soul waits for the LORD more than watchmen

---

[377] Ps. 22:1-2.
[378] Ps. 119:145-150, 153-154.

for the morning.... For with the LORD there is steadfast love, and with him is plenteous redemption."[379]

There might be times when troubles and problems at home overwhelm us. Psalm 4 reminds us, "Answer me when I call, O God of my right! Thou hast given me room when I was in distress. Be gracious to me, and hear my prayer."[380]

There might be times when some are set on making life very difficult on us. Psalm 55 pleads,

Give ear to my prayer, O God; and hide not thyself from my supplication! Attend to me, and answer me; I am overcome by my trouble.... For they bring trouble upon me, and in anger they cherish enmity against me. My heart is in anguish within me.... "O that I had wings like a dove! I would fly away and be at rest.... I would haste to find me a shelter from the raging wind and tempest.... It is not an enemy who taunts me—then I could bear it; it is not an adversary who deals insolently with me—then I could hide from him. But it is you, my equal, my companion, my familiar friend. We used to hold sweet converse together.... I call upon God; and the LORD will save me.... for many are arrayed against me.... I will trust in You.[381]

There might be times when we are falsely accused, and our honest efforts are viewed with suspicion. Psalm 43 fervently prays, "Vindicate me, O God, and defend my cause against an ungodly people; from deceitful and unjust men deliver me! For thou art the God in whom I take refuge; why hast thou cast me off? Why go I mourning because of the oppression of the enemy? Oh send out thy light and thy truth; let them lead me....

---

[379] Ps. 130:1–7.
[380] Ps. 4:1.
[381] Ps. 55:1–4, 6, 8, 12–14, 16, 18, 23.

Why are you cast down, O my soul, and why are you disquieted within me? Hope in God; for I shall again praise hm; my help and my God."[382]

There might be times when someone attempts to spread rumors about us at work. Psalm 5 implores, "Give ear to my words, O LORD; give heed to my groaning. Hearken to the sound of my cry, my King and my God, for to thee do I pray.... Lead me, O LORD, in thy righteousness ... make thy way straight before me.... For thou dost bless the righteous, O LORD; thou dost cover him with favor as with a shield."[383]

There might be times when we are exasperated by some family problems. Psalms 102 beseeches, "Hear my prayer, O LORD; let my cry come to thee! Do not hide thy face from me in the day of my distress! Incline thy ear to me; answer me speedily in the day when I call! For my days pass away like smoke, and my bones burn like a furnace. My heart is smitten like grass, and withered.... I lie awake, I am like a lonely bird on the housetop.... My days are like an evening shadow; I wither away like grass."[384]

There might be times when we are very depressed with what is happening in our personal lives. Psalm 61 exclaims, "Hear my cry, O God, listen to my prayer; from the end of the earth I call to thee, when my heart is faint. Lead thou me to the rock that is higher than I, for thou art my refuge.... Let me dwell in thy tent for ever! Oh to be safe under the shelter of thy wings! For thou, O God, hast heard my vows, thou hast given me the heritage of those who fear thy name."[385]

[382] Ps. 43:1–3, 5.
[383] Ps. 5:1–2, 8, 12.
[384] Ps. 102:1–4, 7, 11.
[385] Ps. 61:1–5.

Why did the inspired Psalmist cry out, "My heart was in anguish"? He indicates that he is present within humanity in a condition not of exaltation but of severe trial. We are no exception to this cry! Our earthly pilgrimage cannot be exempt from trials and challenges.[386] We progress by means of trial or challenge. No one knows himself or herself better except through trial and confronting a challenge. No one receives a crown except after victory. No one strives except against an enemy or temptations. Trials and challenges purify our spiritual lives and our personalities.

In this silence of God, we learn that suffering enlarges our realm of experience at both ends of the scale. When we comprehend pain, we learn to know joy. The first serves as a means for our personality development. Those who endure suffering have the possibility of a richer depth of compassion toward another person's suffering, and therefore they grow as human beings and as people of faith, as Christians.

The understanding of individual payback was foundational to the Psalmists. By the time the Israelites returned from the Babylonian Exile, the shift from the welfare of the community to that of the individual was complete. But, when this law of consequent justice was transferred from the community to the individual, it was clear that experience challenged it at every turn. On the other hand, the Psalmists accepted God's wisdom—God's right to do what He does for whatever reason, and always for the good of the individual—and they recognized their humble stature in comparison to God. Psalm 115 is reminiscent of this message: "Our God is in the heavens; he does whatever he pleases."[387] Thus, there is a larger picture to our individual suffering. This also has personal

---

[386] St. Augustine, *Commentary on Psalm 61*.
[387] Ps. 115:3.

implications when, as in the case of the Psalmists, we cry out to God, who seems to be deaf and blind and silent. They provide us with inspired words to use when speaking with God.

Suffering is an experience that affects our total being: emotional, physical, mental, and spiritual. It brings those whom it controls to moments of critical and agonizing questioning. God accepts and rewards the sincere "hang-on-at-all-costs" fidelity of the sufferer. Jesus knew what it was like to experience the abyss of abandonment, crying out, "Why, God!" — even though Jesus was sinless. The questions of the sufferer are legitimate.

When tragedy strikes, we seem to live in shadows, unacquainted with what is transpiring in the unseen world. The drama that the Psalmists lived through will then replicate itself in our lives; the all-important battle takes place inside us. Will we trust God? Faith is one outcome of a two-pronged decision each sufferer faces. However, when God's silence seems overwhelming, it is at that very moment that the Psalmists experienced that God was disclosing Himself — not totally, but enough. God does not remain silent forever. There is reason to hope for God's presence and answers to cover our needs.

Grief and pain can isolate us from people and from God. Because of the intensity of this aloneness, sufferers may long for the presence of another person. To be present with others in their sufferings is a great gift. There is no need to answer the mysteries of suffering. Our purpose is to share in their sufferings and to show solidarity — nothing more, nothing less. In this regard, the silence of God in the Psalms is crystal clear. He is speechless, but always present.

Why does God appear silent in much of our human sufferings? Perhaps it is because, at times, He is. Though a fearful prospect, the answer to the question may well be that God, in His infinite wisdom, reveals Himself both in word and in silence. God remains in a faithful and constant relationship with us. God's silence is effective in its results in human life. It brings us to a point of decision, a deepened relationship with God, a broadened understanding of who God is, and of our potential glorification. We cannot separate the glory of God-made-Man on the Mount of the Transfiguration from His suffering love on the Mount of Golgotha. The Lord on the first Mount provides a glimpse of what awaits us, while He also shows us on the second Mount how far He goes so that we may see the glory of God. God never fully discloses all the answers to our questions in this life, but, at the same time, God points us to His Son on the Cross. It is there that we are able to find stillness in the midst of much turmoil.

The Silence of God in the New Testament

It was characteristic of pious Jews in ancient times, especially during oppressive eras, to turn their minds and hearts to God and fervently pray for some divine intervention and deliverance. I think we do the same when there is war, or civil unrest, or severe family problems, or problems at work, or a devastating pandemic, and so forth.

When a Jew looked at the entire history of his or her people, that story ascertained that God would eventually intervene and deliver His people from an oppressive ruler or a national catastrophe. They were sure that God never abandoned their nation, His bride.[388] Thus, while the Jewish homeland felt the increasing oppression and weight of the Roman yoke, many faithful Jews prayed more ardently to God to send them a Messiah, a deliverer. They knew that God had been silent since the time of the prophet

---

[388] Isa. 54:5; Jer. 2:2; 31:31–34; Ezek. 16:8–21; Hos. 2:14–16, 19–23.

Daniel and the era of the Maccabees. In other words, we are speaking of about five generations. When we calculate that with today's standards, it means that God had been silent since the time of our grandparents' grandparents. That is a very long time!

Many Jews dreamt about a time of freedom as the Romans governed the Holy Land. Many perceived their new Savior or Messiah in terms of a powerful person who would wield extraordinary political and social powers. In fact, the New Testament tells us of persons who presented themselves as the new leaders of the Jewish nation, only to be defeated by the Romans. Let us recall what Gamaliel said when the first Jewish Christians were denounced to the Sanhedrin, the Jewish religious and civil court: let them be — if this is from God, then we are going against God; if this is from men, then, as has already happened to others, they will disappear.[389] Remember St. John the Baptist sending some of his disciples to ask Jesus "Are you the one?" In other words, are You the long-awaited Savior?

In any case, the Jews around the time of the first Christian century expected God to send them a man who would rise and lead them to freedom from their Roman oppressors and reestablish the kingdom of their great King David. Different incidents in the Gospels indicate to us that even after the apostles had been with Jesus for a long time, they, too, perceived the Messiah and Savior in such terms.

Yet, among the simple people who struggled with the problems of daily life, there were those, the *anawim*, who silently and prayerfully lived in anticipation of the time when God would send His Anointed One to free Israel not from the Romans but from its sins, and to call all Jews to conversion and repentance. From their

[389] Acts 5:34–42.

number came St. Elizabeth and her husband St. Zachariah, and their son St. John the Baptist, old Simeon, the prophetess Anna, and Sts. Joseph and Mary, the Virgin from whom, in the fullness of time, Jesus Christ, the true Messiah, was born.[390] They lived in a faith-filled vigil, waiting for God to break His silence. The New Testament is full of the silence of God.

There is the silence of the Incarnation. We are simply informed that God the Holy Spirit overshadowed Mary and she conceived the Word of God in her virginal womb. God the Father had not spoken directly to Mary. Rather, it was His messenger, the archangel Gabriel, who did so.[391] There is the silence of St. Zachariah, a man who lacked faith and then was given nine months of silence to reflect on this gift of faith. He truly had a deep conversion at the end of his silent retreat, uttering the *Benedictus* at the birth of his son.[392] There is also the silence of God in the Visitation, when the old met the new; the barren become fertile; what was impossible for man was made possible by God in a virginal conception; the recognition by the unborn St. John the Baptist of the presence of God in silence,[393] for the unborn baby did not speak. There is the silence of God in the desert during the temptations of Jesus,[394] for in the desert of prayer and fasting the Lord did not hear the voice of God the Father. There is the silence of God when Jesus turned water into wine at the Wedding in Cana[395]: the miracle was so silent that the servants did not even notice the transformation of water into fine wine. And the steward, instead of rejoicing for

---

[390] Gal. 4:4–7.
[391] Luke 1:26–38.
[392] Luke 1:68–79.
[393] Luke 1:39–56.
[394] Matt. 4:1–11; Mark 1:12–13; Luke 4:1–13.
[395] John 2:1–12.

being spared embarrassment, complained, telling the groom good wine should not be left to the end of the marriage festivities![396]

There is the silence of God at the pool of Siloam, where Jesus healed the blind man.[397] There is the silence of God as Jesus slept in the boat amidst the storm, proving His full humanity, and the apostles thought they were about to sink.[398] Finally, there is the silence of God as Lazarus laid in the silent tomb, while his sisters Mary and Martha wept.[399] Jesus would eventually triumph over that silence by performing the act of resurrecting Lazarus, pointing to our own resurrection, when human epochs stop. We are reminded of what was proclaimed by the prophet Daniel some three centuries before the Savior came down to live in our midst:

> At that time shall arise Michael, the great prince who has charge of your people. And there shall be a time of trouble, such as never has been since there was a nation till that time; but at that time your people shall be delivered, every one whose name shall be found written in the book. And many of those who sleep in the dust of the earth shall awake ... to everlasting life.... Those who are wise shall shine like the brightness of the firmament ... like the stars for ever.[400]

God's silence is not the silent treatment that people give to one another: "I am mad at you; you are no longer important to me; you are not significant enough to be acknowledged by me; you are beneath me; you are not worthy." The silence of God is like a flower seed that grows and blossoms in silence. It has that anticipation

---

[396] John 2:10.
[397] John 9:1–12.
[398] Matt. 8:25; Mark 4:38–40.
[399] John 11:9–16.
[400] Dan. 12:1–3.

similar to one waiting for a phone call. It is like that of two lovers being in each other's presence without uttering one word.

We are very familiar with the scene of the flight to Egypt.[401] God spoke to St. Joseph through a dream, but not to Our Lady, the Mother of the newborn Jesus. He is silent with her, yet she listens to God through St. Joseph. Imagine packing up in a great hurry just after being awakened by your husband and told you must flee the place immediately! Which of your possessions do you take? Which do you leave behind? What is going to happen to your husband's job? Money is short—St. Joseph was a carpenter—and how will you make ends meet? How far away is Egypt? What are you going to do in a strange culture, where people speak a strange language? Where will you find kosher food? Where are you going to stay at night while you're traveling through the desert? Once you get to Egypt, how will Joseph find work?

Here is Jesus, God made man and the Savior of Israel: How is He going to save Israel? Here is the Son of God: things can be easily resolved by God sending death to Herod. Yet He does not do so. Mary's response was very simple: obey God, who has not said one word to her. Yet, she was absolutely certain that God was in an intimate relationship with her. She experienced stillness in God.

Then Mary and St. Joseph were again uprooted: the same traveling questions arose. The same issues about St. Joseph's work arose. Now they had to go to Nazareth. There was some anxiety in relocating again. Yet, God is silent, and Mary's response is the same: move forward in life with absolute faith and trust in God.

There is the silence of God when Jesus was lost in the Temple.[402] We are told that Mary and St. Joseph looked for Him.

---

[401] Matt. 2:13–23.
[402] Luke 2:41–52.

God is silent. He does not tell Mary where to look and alleviate the parents' anxiety about Jesus. They looked, anxious, worried, bewildered. Imagine going to the mall or supermarket and your child simply disappears. You look, you cry, you panic, you ask for help to find your child. This silence of God for those three days of Jesus being lost to His parents anticipates the silence of God when Jesus will be buried in the tomb for three days;[403] and Our Lady did not look for Him in the tomb because she believed He is the Lord of Life. Yet this divine silence brought darkness over the hearts of Mary and St. Joseph. Jesus' parents did not make a bargain with God: "I will be better," or "I will do what You want as long as I find our Son." They were, in fact, following God's will and accepting God's mysterious plan. Their response was simple: live with this darkness, cope with this anxiety, trust God without complaining or asking questions. He is a faithful and loving God.

There is also the silence of God when St. Joseph died. There is no report in the New Testament on when and how he died. What is certain is that Mary was left as a very young widow and Jesus became an orphan.

There is the silence of God the Father when Jesus died on the Cross.[404] Yet that silence speaks volumes. It shows how far God will go as incarnate man to show His love for us. Not only is he willing to die for us: He is willing to die alone. And by that death we are redeemed.

Has God trusted us with His silence—a silence that has great meaning, as was the case with Our Lady, St. Joseph, St. Elizabeth, St. Zachariah, Simeon, and Anna the prophetess? God's silences are actually His answers. Can God trust us with His silence, or

---

[403] Matt. 28:1; Mark 16:1–2; Luke 24:1; John 20:1.
[404] Matt. 27:50; Mark 15:37; Luke 23:46; John 19:30.

are we still asking Him for a visible answer as some Jews asked for a sign in order to believe in Jesus?[405] God's silence is the sign that He is bringing us into an even more wonderful and deeper understanding of Himself.

Are we mourning before God because we have not had an audible response? When we cannot hear God, we will discover that He has trusted us in the most intimate way possible—with absolute silence, not a silence of despair, but one of joy, because He saw that we can withstand an even bigger revelation. If God has given us a silence, then we should praise God, for He is bringing us into the mainstream of His purposes. This is what happened to Our Lady, and to Simeon, who proclaimed, "Mine eyes have seen thy salvation which thou hast prepared in the presence of all peoples."[406]

Remember, too, that our perception of God's responsiveness is warped by our being in time. For time is nothing to God. You or I may say, "I asked God to give me bread, but He gave me a stone instead." In fact, He did not give us a stone, and today we find that He gave us the "Bread of Life."

A wonderful thing about God's silence is that stillness in Him is contagious—it gets into us, hopefully causing us to become perfectly confident so that each one of us can honestly say, "I know that God has heard me." His silence is the very proof that He has heard us. As long as we have the idea that God will always bless us in the best way in answer to our prayer, He will do it. Jesus Christ is bringing us into the understanding that prayer is for glorifying His Father, and He will give us the first sign of His intimacy: silence.

---

[405] Matt. 12:38–39; Mark 8:11–12; Luke 11:16; John 2:18; 6:30.
[406] Luke 2:30-31.

How did St. Peter react to the silent forgiveness that Jesus bestowed on him after he betrayed the Lord? He went away and wept in silence. How did Lazarus react to being called out from the sepulcher of death? In silence he walked out of the tomb. Nicodemus remained silent during the day, but God heard the cry of his weak heart.

The spiritual writer Esther de Waal wrote in chapter three of her book, entitled *Lost in Wonder: Rediscovering the Spiritual Art of Attentiveness,* "Uncrowd my heart, O God, until silence speaks in Your still, small voice; turn me from the hearing of words, and the making of words, and the confusion of much speaking, to listening, waiting, stillness, silence."[407]

Let us listen to the silence of God with tranquil mind and heart. He speaks to us! We seek stillness in our world full of turmoil. We can find it only in our loving and steadfast God.

---

[407] Esther de Waal, *Lost in Wonder: Rediscovering the Spiritual Art of Attentiveness* (Norwich, Norfolk: Canterbury Press, 2003), chap. 3.

Epilogue: God Shutters His Silence

There are instances in the New Testament when God pierces through silence.

There is the scene of Jesus going to the River Jordan to be baptized by John the Baptist. The three Synoptic Gospels relate that as soon as the Lord emerged from the waters, the voice of the Father was heard from the heavens declaring: "This is my beloved Son, with whom I am well pleased."[408] This was not some declaration of Jesus being God's Son by adoption, as was the case with the Jewish kings or the Jewish people or of us at our Baptism. This is a revelation, for the declaration identifies Jesus as the only-begotten Son of the Father, as the second Person of the Blessed Trinity.

There is the scene in the Gospel of St. Matthew when the Lord was speaking with a crowd and a bright cloud overshadowed them and the voice of the Father was heard declaring, "This is my beloved

[408] Matt. 3:17-17; Mark 1:10-11; Luke 3:21-22.

Son, with whom I am well pleased; listen to him."[409] Here was the heavenly Father speaking about His Son and inviting all to listen to Jesus. Eventually, this invitation fell on mostly deaf ears, because in time the Jewish audience found His teachings to be too much for them and departed.[410] Such a scene should evoke in us the reaction of St. Augustine: "You called; You cried; and You broke through my deafness. You flashed, You shone, and You chased away my blindness."[411] Jesus can never be too much for anyone, for what He offers can be matched by no one else.

There is the majestic scene in the Gospel of St. John where Jesus, having been anointed by perfumed oils, speaks with His Heavenly Father about His approaching sufferings and death: "'Now is my soul troubled. And what shall I say? "Father, save me from this hour"? No, for this purpose I have come to this hour. Father, glorify thy name.' Then a voice came from heaven, 'I have glorified it, and I will glorify it again.' The crowd standing by heard it and said that it had thundered. Others said, 'An angel has spoken to him.' Jesus answered, 'This voice has come for your sake, not for mine.'"[412] Note well that the heavenly voice spoke for the benefit of the hearers of Jesus, among whom we number ourselves.

There is the mystical scene of the Transfiguration, narrated in the Gospel of St. Luke. The three intimate apostles, St. Peter, St. James, and his brother St. John, were taken by the Lord to Mount Tabor. Jesus was transfigured in their sight. The Father's voice was heard declaring through the cloud enveloping them: "This is my Son, my Chosen; listen to him!"[413] Well, for sure, one of them did

[409] Matt. 17:5.
[410] John 6:59–71.
[411] St. Augustine, *Confessions*, 10:27.
[412] John 12:27–30.
[413] Luke 12:35, 28–36.

not listen carefully. St. Peter protested with Jesus that He should not undergo His Passion. Are we like St. Peter? Do we want to be with Jesus on the glorious Mount Tabor but not on the excruciating Mount Golgotha?

There are Gospel scenes of the Risen Jesus, whose Resurrection showed that He is truly God, appearing to His disciples and speaking to them, instructing them, eating with them, and being with them in the Upper Room.[414]

There is the scene depicting the Risen Christ appearing again to His disciples in the Upper Room and telling St. Thomas to put his hand in the Lord's hands and in His side wounds to determine that the Risen Christ was not a ghost. Are we more like the doubting St. Thomas seeking proof or like the believing St. Thomas who soon declared Jesus as Lord and God? Or are we perhaps a little of both?

Finally, there is the scene of the Ascension, where the Lord, before returning to the place from which He had come to earth, commissioned His disciples to preach the good news to the whole world, baptizing every person into the household of God.[415] The Great Commission is still in force today and has been issued to us — each and every one of us — at our Baptism. Imagine, the Lord Jesus has entrusted His mission and good news into our frail hands!

I fervently pray that God will break His silence at the moment of our death, when our entire bodies become absolutely silent in earthly matters. Let us pray that each of us hears the voice of God saying to us: "Come, O blessed of my Father, inherit the kingdom prepared for you from the foundation of the world."[416] We, though most unworthy, have been called to eternal glory!

---

414 Matt. 28:1–6; Luke 24:45–48; 24:13–27; John 20:19–23; 21:1–14.
415 Matt. 28:18–20; Mark 16:15; Luke 24:50–53.
416 Matt. 25:34.

About the Author

Born in Malta, Msgr. Laurence Spiteri, J.C.D., Ph.D., was ordained for the Archdiocese of Los Angeles, California. He holds doctorates in biblical studies, psychology, and canon law, and specializes in international law. He serves as prelate auditor of the Roman Rota, is in charge of the legal office of the Vatican Apostolic Library, is a voting member of the Historical Commission at the Dicastery for Causes of Saints, and is CEO of three foundations. He is the author of more than seventy-five books, some of which deal with canon and civil law, as well as of numerous articles. Msgr. Spiteri's works have been published in various languages in the United States, England, Ireland, Malta, Mexico, Portugal, Italy, and Vatican City State.

Sophia Institute

Sophia Institute is a nonprofit institution that seeks to nurture the spiritual, moral, and cultural life of souls and to spread the gospel of Christ in conformity with the authentic teachings of the Roman Catholic Church.

Sophia Institute Press fulfills this mission by offering translations, reprints, and new publications that afford readers a rich source of the enduring wisdom of mankind.

Sophia Institute also operates the popular online resource CatholicExchange.com. *Catholic Exchange* provides world news from a Catholic perspective as well as daily devotionals and articles that will help readers to grow in holiness and live a life consistent with the teachings of the Church.

In 2013, Sophia Institute launched Sophia Institute for Teachers to renew and rebuild Catholic culture through service to Catholic education. With the goal of nurturing the spiritual, moral, and cultural life of souls, and an abiding respect for the role and work of teachers, we strive to provide materials and programs that are at once enlightening to the mind and ennobling to the heart; faithful and complete, as well as useful and practical.

Sophia Institute gratefully recognizes the Solidarity Association for preserving and encouraging the growth of our apostolate over the course of many years. Without their generous and timely support, this book would not be in your hands.

www.SophiaInstitute.com
www.CatholicExchange.com
www.SophiaInstituteforTeachers.org

Sophia Institute Press is a registered trademark of Sophia Institute.
Sophia Institute is a tax-exempt institution as defined by the
Internal Revenue Code, Section 501(c)(3). Tax ID 22-2548708.

Notes

Notes

Notes

Notes